Practices Inspired by the Sutras

The Companion Book to
The Yoga Sutras:
One Woman's Personal, Practical, and Playful Perspective

By D'ana Baptiste

Ordering Information
Quantity sales. Special discounts are available on quantity purchases by yoga studios, schools associations, and non-profit organizations. For details, contact the publisher at d'ana@inbodyacademy.com.Orders by U.S. trade bookstores and wholesalers. Contact the publisher at danabaptisteauthor@gmail.com

Dedication

To all of you who have attended retreats with me. After all these years, what I find most remarkable is that fun and frolic can co-exist with deep transformation.

We've had a lot of fun over the years finding ourselves, haven't we?

And to Kristine, for planting the seeds that brought this book to fruition.

INTRODUCTION

As I was finishing up the more comprehensive book The Yoga Sutras: One Woman's Personal, Practical and Playful Perspective, a close friend (thanks Kris!) suggested I pull the practical bits out to make them even more accessible to the public at large. Arranged in four sections, this is a compilation of observances inspired by the four chapters (padas) found in the Yoga Sutras of Patanjali. Explore the preparation, practicum, powers and potential listed in the Yoga Sutras.

Many people will argue that this is sacrilege; that the secrets from the sutras should only be available to people who can read Sanskrit, who've lived and studied in India, who've followed a guru for years, who've been initiated into secret rituals, etc. My argument has always been "the more people experiencing these deeper practices, the better." There's no better time to incorporate this simple (yet entirely effective) science into your life.

This offering of 52 practices takes them out of context of the definitions that precede and follow them, so this is not a substitute for reading the sutras in entirety. However, this book provides direct access to the practices themselves. My sincere desire is that this compilation will inspire you to take action. Experience a taste of what this science promises. Understand that you can be a totally "normal" person (whatever that means) and still be deeply spiritual. Know that your daily life will provide you with the exact and perfect fodder for your mind to open and your Self to evolve. My hope is that this book will breathe new life into ancient rituals.

I have used the four chapters of Patanjali's Yoga Sutras as a way to organize the chapters of this book, but I have changed the more traditional translations for each chapter.

The working title of Chapter one, for a long time, was "Psychology" because Pada One tells us about the inner workings of our mind. I also liked the title "Science" because Chapter one asserts truths proven scientifically today -- or at least played with in the realm of quantum physics. Ultimately, I entitled the first chapter (Samadhi Pada) "Preparations" because the exercises inspired by it feel like introductory practices, preparing the yogi for the deeper and more subtle practices of the later chapters.

Part of "Preparations" thus includes scientific findings that "back up" the science of the sutras. I included this aspect of the first chapter to prepare the practitioner's mind to more readily accept, and see value in, the practices that follow.

Chapter two is appropriately entitled "Practicum." Patanjali's second chapter, Sadhana Pada, is basically a list of practices, so I stayed pretty true to the translation there, but wanted to imply a need for action, hence the slight change to "Practicum." In other words, you should DO these practices, not just read about them. You'll notice a few of them piggyback on the preparatory exercises of chapter one, with perhaps more detail or subtlety.

Chapter three, entitled "Powers" correlates very well with Patanjali's Vibbhuti Pada, a list of powers. However, the meditations and breathing practices I have chosen to present, are inspired by these sutras, but are not practices that will afford you these powers, per se. Do not expect to levitate after practicing the breathing practice associated with the sutra about levitation!

Chapter four, which I chose to name "Potential" because frankly, I wanted the alliteration, really translates into "Self Realization" or "Freedom." However, the two practices I chose to include in this chapter speak directly to the potential within us self-realize. Only by tapping into that Potential will we uncover our inherent freedom.

The observances, exercises, practices, meditations, and breath work I've chosen to share with you come from many different sources, not just from Patanjali. When a sutra clearly defined a specific observance, I left that practice as is. However, many sutras reminded me of practices I've learned elsewhere, in Reiki training, Kriya initiation, or at a silent vipassana retreat for instance; I've included them in this book as well.

I purposely included 52 practices in hopes that you, the reader, will incorporate one practice per week into your daily life. Try each observance on for a week, keep it if it made a difference, or drop it and move on to the next exercise. Some require you to sit still and close your eyes, but many observances engage your mind as you engage in your life. They can, if you encourage them, become new and powerful habits. If you find a practice that obviously works for you, give yourself the gift of 40 days of daily practice to really create a lasting edifying habit.

I also love the idea of people using this book as a way to exercise their intuition. Set an intention or ask a question, open the book, and let the Universe decide which practice is best for you in that moment.

Finally, know that this is not an exhaustive list of practices; rather, these are most of my personal favorites, many of which I present at my retreats and in my teacher certification programs. They work. I use them myself. I get joy from them. They have changed the way I approach this lifetime and I hope they will enhance your life as well. Enjoy and have fun!

Chapter One
Preparation

"The only way that we can live is if we grow. The only way that we can grow is if we change. The only way that we can change is if we learn. The only way we can learn is if we are exposed. And the only way that we can become exposed is if we throw ourselves out into the open. Do it. Throw yourself."
~ C. Joy Bell

#1 making breath an object

1:17 The settled mind itself is known as "Samadhi." Samprajnata Samadhi is a meditation that requires an object.

Samprajnata Samadhi is a meditation that requires an object. We will use the breath for our object of awareness, but you can use any object.

1) Sit on a chair with both feet on the ground. Focus on your breath.

2) Feel your cogitation/reasoning mind settle. You'll notice your thoughts start to have space between them. Allow the breath to become less important.

3) Then you will feel reflective. You'll feel as though you're gazing in a mirror that shares information without stories or words. You're still receiving information but it's more present moment; it's quiet, it's subtle. Allow the breath to stop informing you.

4) Then a feeling of bliss unattached to any form. You'll sense a rejoicing, a certain content anticipation, as you approach your true nature. Let go of the object altogether.

5) Meet with pure I-AM-ness. Abide in your true nature.

This a circular experience. You won't just go through the cycle once and then abide in pure being-ness for the rest of the time that you're practicing. You'll notice the thoughts arising again, then the space between the thoughts, then the subtle sinking further toward Source, then exhilaration, then Samadhi for maybe a longer period of time . . . with thoughts arising as the process cycles through again.

ALL FOUR PARTS of the process are worthy of attention. ALL four steps are steps of Samadhi. All four stages are priming the mind, as this process connects us again and again to the medial prefrontal cortex as we meditate. Object-based meditation also makes it more likely that we will access the medial prefrontal cortex in our daily lives even when we are NOT meditating. We are literally and functionally changing our minds.

The way we do this is by "leaving residue" or "creating latent impressions" for the mind to follow in an easier way the next time. Kind of like leaving a trail of breadcrumbs that we follow to make a pathway.

The pathway eventually becomes a paved road, which then becomes a highway. These are the samskaras or "scars" we choose to carve upon the field of mind, rather than those we've habitually yet unconsciously strengthened. Remember that samskaras in this context aren't "bad" or something we want to avoid.

Meditation practitioners demonstrated greater functional connectivity within the DMN in the medial prefrontal cortex area than did controls.
These results suggest that the long-term practice of meditation may be associated with functional changes in regions related to internalized attention even when meditation is not being practiced.
~ Buddha's Brain, Neuroplasticity and Meditation

#2 isvara pranidhana

1:28 Repeat the sound OM constantly, and let it absorb your attention. Om's essence will be realized as you repeat it.

1) Inhale, then while exhaling chant "om" out loud (at least ten times).

2) Inhale, and as you exhale whisper OM, quietly, at least ten times.

3) Inhale and as you exhale repeat OM internally, at least ten times.

4) Finally, experience the essence of OM, abide there.

 When the mind wanders again, start over.

This is one of my FAVORITE meditations. It's easy and effective. I challenge you to try it for ten days in a row, twice a day. This reduces suffering because it redirects our focus away from personal "problems" and issues that make us feel self - obsessed and dramatic.

"The high-amplitude pattern of gamma synchrony in expert meditators during an emotional version of OM meditation support the idea that the state of OM may be best understood in terms of a succession of dynamic global states. Compared to a group of novices, the adept practitioners self-induced higher-amplitude sustained electroencephalography (EEG) gamma-band oscillations and long-distance phase synchrony, in particular over lateral fronto-parietal electrodes, while meditating. Importantly, this pattern of gamma oscillations was also significantly more pronounced in the baseline state of the long-term practitioners compared with controls, suggesting a transformation in the default mode of the practitioners. Although the precise mechanisms are not clear, such synchronizations of oscillatory neural discharges may play a crucial role in the constitution of transient networks that integrate distributed neural processes into highly ordered cognitive and affective functions."

#3 ishvara pranidhana, I AM

1:28 Repeat the sound OM constantly, and let it absorb your attention. Om's essence will be realized as you repeat it.

I learned this from Wayne Dyer, who took his inspiration from Moses in the Old Testament. He witnessed that God's name was I AM. This form of the OM meditation comes from the premise that "I AM" is the sound of God.

1) Inhale, then while exhaling chant out loud "I AM" (at least ten times).

2) Inhale, and as you exhale whisper I AM, quietly, at least ten times.

3) Inhale, and as you exhale repeat I AM silently, at least ten times.

4) Finally, experience the essence of I AM, abide there until the mind wanders again. And then begin again.

Don't let it escape you that Patanjali refers to "I-AM-ness" in meditation #1 from sutra 1:17.

I am Alpha and Omega,
the beginning and the end,
the first and the last.
~ Revelations 22:13

#4 citta saha-bhuvah

1:30 There are nine kinds of obstacles (mental distractions) naturally encountered on the path towards devotion:
1) **Sickness/Disease**
2) **Mediocrity/procrastination**
3) **Doubt/indecision**
4) **Lack of attention to presence/negligence**
5) **Laziness/lethargy**
6) **Failing to turn away from the world/cravings for pleasure**
7) **False perception/delusion**
8) **Failing to gain a higher ground/inability to become**
9) **Slipping from the ground gained/instability**

This list, as Patanjali states, is a list of habits or patterns -- to which all humans are prone -- that get in the way of experiencing yoga (experience yoga = abide in true nature). The next sutra tells us how to recognize when we have fallen into one of these habits.

1:31 From these obstacles, there are four consequences that arise:
1) **DUHKHA: pain**
2) **DAUR-MANASYA: frustration, depression, fatigue**
3) **ANGAM-EJAYATVA: shakiness, anxiety, unsteadiness of limbs**
4) **SVASA-PRA-SVASAH: Irregularities of breath, disturbed breath**

These PHYSICAL indicators give us a "heads up." Physical pain, physical fatigue, physical shakiness, and physical irregularities of breath.

1:32 To counteract this, absorb your attention into one object.

If we take the three sutras (1:30 – 1:32) together then:
step one: awareness of the obstacle. Check in with your body and emotions.

step two: observation of the tangible physical markers. Notice the signs.

step three: decision to bring the mind to a single focus. Focus on the tangible sensations.

Clearly, we have free agency and a way to neutralize and counteract our tendency to stay in a state where we aren't connected to Source. Thus . . . when the above physical indices arise in the body, make them into objects of your awareness. Bring ALL your attention there.

By bringing all of your attention to that state, you'll notice you begin to put space between sensation and Self. You'll still feel it, but you'll understand that you are NOT the feeling. Your body temporarily experiences pain or fatigue or unsteadiness or irregularities. Attending to these seemingly "negative" sensations makes them objects; once you see them as objects you truly understand their temporary nature.

When your body feels receptive and expansive, or energetic and alive, or steady and strong, or the breath feels very regular, use these feelings as objects of your awareness. The same outcome will ensue; eventually, you'll be prompted back to Source.

Your consciousness will learn an extremely profound truth: that sensation is simply sensation, it is not good or bad, and it is not YOU. It is--simply stated-- object, rather than subject.

1. Focus on the sensation as the "object of your attention."

2. Watch the thoughts that come up around that sensation.

3. Then watch the space between the thoughts.

4. Watch your mind become reflective and the sensation subside.

5. Then feel a feeling of elation.

6. When the mind begins to wander, repeat.

Growth is possible when one is able to reflect upon something in a fresh light and subsequently come to understand it in a different way, that is to take something that was once Subject and make it Object. That which is Subject includes emotions, assumptions, beliefs, and the other ways in which people create meaning in their lives that are hidden within the subconscious. As a result, people are unknowingly shaped by and are unable to objectify these elements. In contrast, that which is Object are those elements currently available to our conscious mind, and as such, we are aware of them, able to reflect on them, and able to be in control of them. Moving an element from Subject to Object, that is, objectifying something to which one was previously subject, fuels cognitive development, in that the more one takes as Object, the more one can appreciate and understand, and the more complex one's overall outlook.
~ Kegan amd Solms, 1994 and 2014

#5 citta pra-sadanam

1:33 The "mind-stuff" is pacified by cultivating feelings of friendliness toward the joyful, compassion for those who are suffering, delight for the virtuous and neutrality toward those we experience as without merit.

When you notice that you need a distraction, or are already distracted, use people around you to practice presence. Choose any person within your vicinity and feel one of these feelings instead.

If you find a joyful person, cultivate friendliness.

If you find someone who is suffering, cultivate compassion.

If you find a virtuous person, cultivate wonder.

If you find an unlikeable person, cultivate neutrality.

Try it. It focuses your mind outside of yourself (thus answering the "need" for distraction) but because you focus on cultivating one feeling, the consequence of anxiety – thus need for distraction -- will disappear. It's cool. And it works pretty quickly.

Your mind chatter stills once you focus on one feeling. So if you want to silence the cacophony in your head, this is one way to do so; not only is it fun but it shows your mind that you have the ability to decide what to feel. As we use our conscious mind in this way, over time we create and fortify new neural pathways. Or in "yoga-speak" we "leave *samskara;*" i.e, leave residue, latent impressions, or scars on the field of the mind. Remember that scars in this context aren't "bad" or something we want to avoid. We decide what to "impress" upon our mind.

Functional MRI studies have implicated the medial prefrontal cortex and temporoparietal junction as important brain regions in theory of mind. These regions are active during complex interconnected mental concepts such as the representation of another individual's actions, desires, and belief systems, the formulation and judgment of other's perspectives, and the inhibition of actions.
~McCleery, 2011, Gweon, 2013, Bowman, 2017.

#6 bahir khumbaka

1:34 The mind is also calmed by breathing practices that include breath retention after full exhalations.

When you notice, for example, that you've been in your head making up stories, notice your breath is choppy or shaky as a result. Change the pattern of your breath, take the breath off auto-pilot, and focus solely on breathing differently. This Sutra defines the practice of exhaling all of the air out of your body and then holding the out breath.

1) Take a full breath in.

2) Exhale all the air out.

3) Hold empty for as long as you can.

4) When you're ready to take another inhale, inhale slowly, pause for a moment in the fullness of the in breath, then exhale naturally before beginning again.

5) Repeat at least ten times.

Notice how quickly you get out of your head and your storytelling. You'll step into your body and will feel the presence of breath, the presence of attention, and the settling of the mind into the void of non-breath. It seems so simple, but how often do you actually do this? Try it. Do it. Often.

If you have trouble sleeping, this is a good breathing practice to do in bed, but without the longer holds. Exhale for as long as you can, hold empty for a conscious moment, allow the inhale to come in (it will be shorter than the exhale, that's fine) and then take the longest most complete exhale possible again. Usually, ten repetitions will calm the mind and allow you to get some shut-eye.

"This is important information for anyone struggling to manage his or her emotional life. When caught up in the intensity of an emotion, particularly the so-called "negative" emotions — anger, sadness, fear and its low-lying cousin anxiety, it is difficult to observe one's own breathing pattern. But to a detached observer the patterns are obvious. When we're sad we sigh frequently. When angry, we breathe rapidly. In the grip of fear our breathing is shallow and from the top of the lungs. And sometimes we hold our breath without realizing that's what we're doing. . . . But the element of our emotions that we can manage by ourselves is breathing."
~Philippot, P. & Blairy, S. 2010.

#7 pravritti

1:35 The natural inclination to pay attention to your senses can also encourage tranquility of the mind; use it to practice sensing your more subtle and extraordinary perceptions.

I use this particular practice to hone my skills as a yoga therapist. Once I practice subtle and extraordinary perception of my own sensations, I'm more likely to tune in and be present with others' subtle and deeper feelings. You know this works because you know you've done it unconsciously. Practicing this in a conscious way is even more powerful.

Without any expectations, set a timer for ten minutes. For the next ten minutes, simply absorb your attention into your senses. You'll then notice there are more subtle sensations; absorb your attention into these subtle sounds, feelings, smells, tastes, and/or perceptions. The fluctuations of your mind will still. That's cool enough. But you're also building skills in becoming extraordinarily aware of prompts that are always there; you just haven't noticed them yet.

Since we're naturally inclined to turn toward our senses, this sutra suggests using those inclinations as a prompting to practice concentration. Right now I am sitting outside in Mexico, typing these words. If I broaden my awareness, I notice the sound of the ocean, the sound of sweeping, the sound of shoveling, the sound of children laughing and screaming in the river, the sound of boats starting up. I can focus on these sounds together or choose one sound to concentrate on. When I do, I begin to notice more subtle sounds; quieter sounds. Birds ruffling their feathers, or lizards scurrying through the rocks, I can now hear more of what has always been there. This works with any of your senses.

"The goal of every living brain, no matter what its level of neurological sophistication, from the tiny knots of nerve cells that govern insect behavior on up to the intricate complexity of the human neocortex, has been to enhance the organism's chances of survival by reacting to raw sensory data and translating it into a negotiable rendition of a world… None of [our] quintessentially human accomplishments would have been possible without the brain's ability to generate rich, effective, and meaningful perceptions of the world."
~Andrew Newberg, M.D. Why God Won't Go Away

#8 citta jyoti

1:36 Stilling the mind is achieved by fixing the gaze on inner radiance.

This particular practice, when done consistently, stills the mind quickly and easily; over time it instills a sense of peace in your day even when you aren't actively practicing. Here are a few ways to connect to inner radiance:

1) Kriya Yoga teaches that "light resides in the spine", so you can use your spine as a starting point. Sit in meditation pose, upright, close your eyes and look for the vertebrae of your spine, then look for radiance inside the spine. Once you find any hint of light, continue to observe it.

2) OR in seated pose, try focusing on your third eye center (Ajna chakra) by gazing at the very center of your brain. Make sure to keep your physical eyes relaxed. Notice any light that seems to fill your skull or move upward beyond the confines of your skull.

3) OR, in a seated pose, imagine that you are gazing down from directly above your spine, from the vantage point of the inside of the crown of your head, noticing whatever radiance is flowing from your crown and down into your spine.

4) If you're tired, lie down, cover your eyes with your palms (lightly) and just watching the light show behind your eyelids. When your arms get tired, let them rest alongside the body. Keep your focus on any evidence of light or electricity, color or static you may experience.

Neurophysiologic changes as measured through electroencephalography have also been shown to occur as meditators bring awareness to themselves, with distinct differences in EEG profiles depending on experience. For example, a study on Satyananda Yoga practitioners demonstrated that intermediate practitioners with a mean experience of 4 years had increased low frequency oscillations (theta and alpha) in the right superior frontal, right inferior frontal and right anterior temporal lobes, whereas advanced practitioners with a mean experience of 30 years had increased high frequency oscillations (beta and gamma) in the same regions. ~Thomas et al, 2014

#9 citta raja

1:37 Or by directing consciousness toward the heart of an "illumined soul."
I love to read about great human beings and superhuman beings and am inspired
by the heart of Jesus and Buddha for instance. If you enjoy studying anyway, I
highly recommend experimenting with this.

1. Read about the heart of one illumined soul a day for 30 days.

2. Become aware of feelings of lightness, buoyancy, and expansion.

3. Use both the specific inspiration (of the individual) and the general
feeling of "largeness" as you objects of awareness.

4. Notice that this contemplation has led you to a state where you abide in
the same nature you admire about that "illumined soul." This will lead you
to a feeling of bliss.

5. Notice your mind making up stories; this is your signal to begin the
process again.

This pro-active form of concentration proves to our subconscious that we do have
within us the same traits and lightness of being that our esteemed "illumined
souls" have. We cultivate these traits by focusing on them. It allows us to feel these
feelings so that we know how to make them stronger within us.

Remember you're not out to "achieve" anything. This practice stills your mind and
takes you off of auto-pilot. It trains your attention to focus on feelings. The practice
helps you re-learn how to feel; admiration and openness, inspiration and
buoyancy. And it prompts your experience into an "altered state." Ultimately we
learn that we can indeed alter our state of mind easily.

#10 svapna jnana

1:38 Or, another way to interrupt habitual patterns is to witness the process of dreaming.

Use your dreams as the object of your one-pointed attention. This could mean a few things, and again if we are willing to experiment with these we find that the attempt itself starts to build new neural pathways and connections. Try any or all of these options separately OR gradually build the skills from 1 - 6 until you are lucid dreaming.

1. Set an intention before you go to sleep, to dream about something specific. Train your mind to dream.

2. Ask a question and ask your dreams to work out the answer while you are within the dream itself. When you wake, have a notebook and pen waiting to record any insights.

3. The practice of simply remembering your dreams is an educational tool as well. Again, keep a notebook and pen right next to your bed, and as soon as you wake, while in that "in-between" state, write down as much detail of the dream as possible. I recommend writing the major details first -- so double or even triple space your first "memories" of the dream -- then go back and fill in the details. If writing wakes you too quickly, try making an audio recording instead.

4. While you're dreaming, notice more details within the dream. Is it in color or black and white? Are there words or numbers you can detect? Is the location a brand new place or a place you've returned to? Can you see faces clearly or are they blurred?

5. Simply pull back from the dream you are having and slow it down as if it is a   instead of a movie. This will begin to train your unconscious to "lucid dream."

6. Lucid dreaming, or the decision to remark to yourself--while dreaming--that you are in fact dreaming. You decide to take a more active role in the dreamlike deciding to fly into the air or walk through a wall – or decide to actively change the outcome of the dream.

A group of scientists in Germany found that "self-reflection in everyday life is more pronounced in persons who can easily control their dreams. The area of the brain responsible for self-reflection (among others) is significantly larger among lucid dreamers." Lucid dreaming can help in overcoming nightmares and sharpen creativity and problem-solving skills. Once you know you are dreaming, you can do basically anything your mind can imagine without obeying the laws of society and physics.

#11 yoga nidra

1:38 Focus on the nature of the state of dreamless sleep as another way to still the mind.

In this interpretation, the practice that will help you discover the nature of dreamless sleep (and I will call it the hypnogogic state) is yoga nidra. It is a multi-layered process derived from an ancient tantric practice and it should be something you do with a guide. There are many podcasts and downloads you can access from your computer or smart-phone, but it's not a practice you can get through alone. When finding a yoga nidra practice to attend or to download, look for the following elements:

1. Internalization: Make sure your teacher/guide first does something to bring you into your interior state. This could be doing a few yoga poses or some breath work, and then setting you up in a comfortable prone position and prompting you to go inside.
2. You'll be asked to create a sankalpa; basically, a mantra that you will repeat and insert into different layers of the physical and subtle bodies as your guide prompts.
3. Your teacher will lead you through your entire physical body, asking you to bring awareness to the physical layer.
4. You'll be asked to repeat your sankalpa.
5. Your teacher will lead you through a breath awareness exercise to bring attention to your breath layer.
6. You'll be prompted to repeat your sankalpa, your resolve.
7. Your teacher will have you manufacture opposite feelings (physical, mental and emotional) to help bring awareness to your mental layer.
8. Repetition of your sankalpa.
9. Your guide will call out certain images and prompt you to visualize them so that awareness shines on your intelligence layer.
10. Repetition of your personal sankalpa.
11. Your guide will lead you in an exercise to bring awareness to the bliss layer of the body. This will induce a feeling of limitlessness.
12. Repeat resolve once again.

13. Externalization: Your teacher will take the time to bring you back into your physical body and the limitations of the body. This may be done with deep breaths or yoga poses or shaking of the limbs or other movements. Once you've moved through these layers, you should take your time moving into the next thing you are doing, whatever it is.

In the practice of Yoga Nidra, we look to reach the Hypnagogic state – the state between waking a dreaming in which the ego-mind isn't as in control as it might usually be. When we're in the Hypnagogic state, we're able to relax even more than we might do when sleeping. This state of being is also known as 'creative surrender', as it is a deliberate and conscious relaxation of the mind and body. When we reach this state, we surrender and open up to reality, creating space in the mind for reality to flow through. The hypnagogic state sheds light on how our thought processes can be very different when we're truly relaxed than when we're in our usual mindset. It is said that the hypnagogic state is one in which there is a 'loosening of ego boundaries' and creative ideas are more fluid.
~Emma Newlyn

#12 open monitoring (om)

1:39 Peace can also be reached by concentrating on whatever is appealing, agreeable, or attractive; that which is dearest to the heart.

I adore this sutra. After a long list of practices, the last suggestion given is "or hey, just pay attention to whatever. It doesn't matter as long as it holds your attention." WHAT? How simple is that? Concentrate on the waves of the ocean, the ticking of a clock, the lizard on the ceiling. Fix your attention on your child, your own body, your hand. Whatever. The point is . . . practice being present with everything because nothing that is attracting our attention is too small for us, and it is all here for us to use as an object of our awareness. Fully notice and feel, see and perceive, listen and hear the essence of whatever it is you are choosing to attend to.

This is an example of "Open Monitoring" Meditation: The stairs I walk daily to and from the beach require my full attention. I've started to get to know each step and have even named a few of them. One is tall and wide, another only half covered with cement so one side is higher than the other. The next step is so short your toes hang off it, and the next step shallow enough to have me teetering precariously for a moment. The next step feels deep in comparison. As though I'm stepping into an abyss. Then the stair seems to rise up and meet my bare foot, reassuring my body that it was there all along. Each stair offers itself up to me to be known and seen and understood. Each step requires my full presence. The stairwell, a mish-mash of personalities, the very opposite of "formula," keeps my mind checked in. This to me is the perfect walking meditation and a great example of using anything you encounter as your object of concentration.

I invite you to resolve to practice in this way for at least a week. Choose some experience you do every day; perhaps you have stairs to climb daily as well – and decide that this will be the moment you choose to "open monitor." Let it be something appealing or agreeable to you; something that naturally draws your attention.

For me, in the example above, I chose to use the experience of walking the stairs to and from the beach. Every day I walked the stairs I resolved to stay aware of all sensations, to notice everything there was to notice about the simple experience of walking down – and back up at the end of the day – the stairs.

The Focused Attention (FA) meditation entails voluntary focusing attention on a chosen object in a sustained fashion.

The Open Monitoring (OM) meditation involves non-reactively monitoring the content of experience from moment-to-moment, primarily as a means to recognize the nature of emotional and cognitive patterns.

OM meditation initially involves the use of FA training to calm the mind and reduce distractions, but as FA advances, the cultivation of the monitoring skill per se becomes the main focus of practice. The aim is to reach a state in which no explicit focus on a specific object is retained; instead, one remains only in the monitoring state, attentive moment-by-moment to anything that occurs in experience. These two common styles of meditation are often combined, whether in a single session or over the course of practitioner's training.

~Buddha's Brain: Neuroplasticity and Meditation

#13 candle gazing

1.42 **savitarka samadhi: the mind achieves identity with a gross object of concentration and can still name it and know the quality of it.**
1.43 **nirvitarka samadhi: the mind is quiet enough to be absorbed in attention without attachment to the form of the gross object.**
1.44 **In the same way we can focus on gross objects, we can use subtle objects.**
savichara samadhi: the mind achieves identity with a subtle object of concentration, and can still name it and know the quality of it.
nirvichara samadhi: the mind has stilled enough to be absorbed in attention without attachment to the form of the subtle object.

These sutras clarify the terms "gross" and "subtle" and remind us of the gradations of gross and subtle. This is not a sorting; it is not an either/or situation. Gross leads into subtle and subtle leads into pure potentiality.
Thus, while anything in "form" is considered a gross object, a candle is grosser than the flame. And while the light from the flame is considered a subtle object, the light you see when you close your eyes after concentrating on the light of the flame is even subtler. One of many ways you can experiment with this hypothesis is to use the candle. I first practiced this meditation technique with Indra Devi.

1) Find a candle and place it on a table with nothing else on the table. Light the candle and sit in a chair with both feet on the ground.

2) Direct all of your attention to the candle. Notice your mind will become absorbed in the flame.

3) Close your eyes and see the flame with your mind's eye.

4) See your own inner light.

5) Experience the feeling of absorption into light itself. As your awareness absorbs into light, consciousness dissolves into this indefinable place/space where anything is possible but where there is nothing AT ALL to cling to as an "object." You're completely FREE of the candle, the flame, the light from the flame, the light within, and even the idea of light.

Neuroplasticity is a term that is used to describe the brain changes that occur in response to experience. There are many different mechanisms of neuroplasticity ranging from the growth of new connections to the creation of new neurons. When the framework of neuroplasticity is applied to meditation, we suggest that the mental training of meditation is fundamentally no different than other forms of skill acquisition that can induce plastic changes in the brain.
~Poldrack, 2002.

Chapter Two
Practicum

"Even a little practice of this yoga will save you from the terrible wheel of rebirth and death"
~Bhagavad Gita 2:40

#14 kapalabhati

2:1 The preliminary or practical steps on the path of yoga are called Kriya yoga. There are three components:

1) intensity through purifying the senses (*tapas*) Swami Nirmalananda Giri adds: "Tapas literally means 'to generate heat' in the sense of awakening or stimulating the whole of our being to higher consciousness . . . Basically, tapas is spiritual discipline that produces a perceptible result, particularly in the form of purification....whenever tapas is spoken of it always implies the practice of yoga and the observances that facilitate yoga practice."

2) refinement through self-study/study (*svadyaya*) Raquel Alexandra, a modern-day blogger yogi, uses the term "cultivating the witness consciousness." She refers to it with great imagery: "it's helpful for me to maintain an image of . . . my Self as a quiet fly on the wall, watching the thoughts of this woman . . ."

3) complete surrender into the creative source from which we emerged (*Isvara pranidhana*) As B.K.S. Iyengar describes it: "Through surrender the aspirant's ego is effaced, and . . . grace . . . pours down upon him like a torrential rain."

This sutra -- the first sutra in the chapter of "action" -- can best be described as "preparation." It may well be stating, "Here's how to ready your body (purify your senses), your mind (study and self-study), and your spirit (surrender to Isvara) to receive the gift that is yoga."

I've chosen one of my favorite practices to exemplify all three of these components: Kapalabhati, or "skull shining breath." A traditional internal cleansing technique, it builds heat (tapas), allows you to bear witness to the machinations of your mind (svadyaya), and encourages a feeling of surrender to Grace (isvara pranidhana).

1.   Notice your breath. Make sure that when you exhale you feel your abdominal muscles draw inward. If your exhale pushes your lower belly out, work ONLY on step one until the exhale contracts your lower abs. Place your hand on the belly (between the pubis and the navel) to make sure it draws IN on exhale.

2.   Once you've found that, begin to take more active exhalations. Follow the exhale all the way to empty. The exhale should take at least 6 seconds, followed by an inhale of at least three seconds. Take ten breaths that way. Train the abs to engage with each long exhale. After ten long exhalations, let the mind settle for a moment.

3.   Change your exhale to make it short, explosive, and staccato. The exhale will last less than a second. Take ten of these exhales with the mouth open. The belly will "rebound" after every exhale, so no need to consciously inhale. Keep your hand on your belly to make sure the out breath still engages the abs. After ten with mouth open, stop, take an active inhalation, hold it for a moment, then follow with a "passive" exhale.

4.   Finally, close the mouth but keep the out breath fast and rhythmic (exhale for no longer than one second). Do ten repetitions (work your way up to more slowly), then take an inhale through the nose, hold it for a moment, letting it go with a passive exhalation.

5.   Repeat step four ten times, for a total of 100 repetitions. Eventually, you'll be able to do the 100 in one cycle, but work up to it! After 100, take a moment (or longer, if you have it) to let the breathing practice drop away. Simply sit with the essence of what your devotion cultivated. This prepares your mind for meditation.

#15 counter impressions

2:10 When the klesas are in their potential state or "subtle form", they can be overcome by producing counter impressions in the mind to still the mind.

We know that where we direct our attention defines us on a neurological level. What we repeatedly think about and where we focus our attention is what we neurologically become. This active practice helps focus our consciousness on whatever presents itself throughout the day. The klesas will be the objects you notice; that noticing will "trigger" you into reframing what you're focusing on.

The klesas are root obstacles on the path of self realization
avidya = forgetting who you are
asmita = identifying with ego
raga = attachment
dvesha = aversion
abhinivesha = fear of death / fear of change

1.   Pick one obstacle (klesa) to work with and commit to use it as a wake up call for just one day. I'll pick "attachment" as the one to discuss.

2.   Whenever you notice any inklings of attachment, let that feeling remind you to consciously produce a different impression for yourself. For example, when you feel attachment come up, create an image in your mind indicative of detachment. Feel the feeling of letting go, as you visualize yourself letting go of something.

3.   Reframe it as an opportunity to practice the art of letting go. It doesn't need to correspond to the thing you are attached to. Maybe you can't let a thought go; notice that you're grasping at this thought, but simultaneously create a picture in your mind of letting a balloon go, or putting down a heavy weight and walking away.

This sounds silly, but it's about interrupting a pattern. When you witness your mind planting the seeds of potential obstacles, use that as a reminder to instead plant a seed of equanimity.

When weeds haven't yet appeared above the surface of the earth, you can plant flowers or strawberries or snap peas. Instead of feeding the weeds, you fertilize what you placed in the field deliberately. In this way you resolve the potential weeds back to their un-manifested origin (undifferentiated matter). What you consciously planted takes up the space where otherwise weeds would grow.

#16 klesa diffusion

2:11 When the klesas are in active form, they can be diffused by meditation.

When the weeds (the root causes of suffering) have grown tall, the above practice won't be enough, because the habit – the klesha -- is too well established. It has become a blind spot, in a sense. We can't see the forest for the trees. There are of course many meditations to practice; one of my favorites is a simple one I learned when I was twenty two years old.

1) Sit on a chair with both feet on the ground.

2) Let the backs of your hands rest on each thigh with your palms face up.

3) With your eyes closed, as though you're looking through the center of your forehead, gaze down at your palms.

4) When your mind starts to wander away from your palms, bring your attention back to your hands and start to gaze at each finder in turn.

5) From the pinkies look at the ring fingers, the middle fingers, the index fingers, and then the thumbs. Cycle back from the thumbs to the pinkies.

6) When and if the mind wanders from this task, come back to it but add counting. Start with one at the pinky, move to five at the thumb, and then count down from the thumbs to one at the pinkies again. Practice this for ten minutes a day, three times a day, or whenever you notice you've encountered a blind spot.

#17 love list

2:14 These seeds produce pleasure or pain according to their original cause.

Life experiences cause pleasure or pain depending on the quality of their original intent.

Bruce Lipton suggests in his book The Biology of Belief that our cells respond to feelings of pleasure and joy with regenerative growth, while fear, hatred or anger causes them to shrink and retreat, allowing disease to take hold. Put another way then, we could say that these seeds regenerate or degenerate according to the character of the matter we originally used to form them.

My friend Missy and her habit of going to bars illustrate this well. Missy felt compelled to take a journal to bars by herself on a regular basis. She'd pick a spot where she could observe people, order a beer, and write down everything she loved about everyone she saw. Her intention generated ease in the world, thus her habit produced joy. Had she habitually gone to the bar to black out or to write what she hated about people in her journal, that life experience would have generated disease in the world and would have caused sorrow.

You can do this simple practice throughout your day or days. Carry a notebook with you. When you think of someone, and have a feeling of love, friendship, appreciation or compassion for them, write their name down. It's that easy.

#18 yama observance

2:30 The Yamas are vows of self-restraint, refusals, abstentions.

1. **Ahimsa - Non-harming, Non-violence**
2. **Satya - Non-lying, Non-falsehood**
3. **Asteya - Non-stealing, Non-theft**
4. **Bramacharya - Non-using, Non-indulgence**
5. **Aparigraha - Non-clinging, Non-Greed, Non-attachment**

All the yamas apply to actions, words and thoughts. They acknowledge that humans have within them the tendency to harm, to lie, to steal, to over-indulge, and to cling. We've all been faced with at least the temptation to engage in all of these actions; most of us have done them all, and some of us are well established in at least one of these tendencies.

Remember that this is one of the eight practices we engage in to polish and purify our inner gaze so that we may see clearly. They are not commandments to regulate morality; rather they are EXERCISES to free the Self. These are ACTIONS, not ideals. They are specific REFUSALS rather than general goals.

This list is stated in the negative (non-) for a reason, suggesting that we are absolutely able -- when faced with the opportunity to act in those ways – to choose NOT to. Abstention from habitual or even unconscious tendencies requires more presence and greater specificity. Instead of saying "vow always to be kind" the sutra says simply "when faced with the option to hurt something/someone, choose not to do it."Let that sink in for a moment. This has been one of the most important distinctions in my life; it's easy to gloss over because it's such a simple concept.

Each time we face dilemmas, we're afforded another opportunity to choose differently, thus making stronger the tendency to engage consciously; bring our choices into the conscious realm. Therefore, even the temptation to lie, cheat or steal can be seen in a positive light. It gives us yet another opportunity to exercise our free agency while fortifying new habits. These specific choices cultivate kindness, truthfulness, respect, integrity, and generosity, eventually they become our new temptations.

This list of five awareness exercises should be practiced spontaneously when these traits come up to be noticed. When faced with real life challenges, take yourself off of autopilot to build new habits and hone new skills.

Ahimsa - Non-harming, Non-violence. When you're tempted to hurt someone or something, notice that and choose to not harm.

Satya - Non-lying, Non-falsehood. When given the opportunity to lie, notice that and choose to not lie.

Asteya - Non-stealing, Non-theft. When you could get away with stealing, notice that and choose to not steal.

Bramacharya - Non-using, Non-indulgence. When faced with the option to use something / someone, notice that and choose to not use.

Aparigraha - Non-clinging, Non-Greed, Non-attachment. When you could hoard and cling to your belongings, notice that and choose to not cling.

#19 pratipaksa bhavanam

2:33 pratipaksa- bhavanam (cognitive reframing): When thoughts contrary to yoga arise, cultivate the opposite thoughts.
2:34   Thoughts contrary to yoga bring certain suffering, whether committed by oneself, caused by others or condoned in others; whether motivated by greed, anger, or falsehood; whether they be mild, moderate, or intense. Hence the necessity of pondering upon the opposites.

1. For this exercise, rather than keeping it open-ended as an all day observance, sit quietly and simply witness your thoughts for 20 minutes. When you observe thoughts, you quickly realize that some thoughts or beliefs are ridiculous and outdated. This simple realization begins to loosen the chains that bind you to that belief system, putting you back in the driver's seat of your own mind.

2. At that moment, in real time, ponder the opposite of that thought pattern so that you now use your mind to program thoughts that you've chosen to think, rather than those programmed into you long ago.

3. When you realize a thought motivated by greed, fear, anger, insecurity, etc. is NOT ACCURATE, take a proactive role in your thought process to reduce suffering for yourself and others.

4. Try this once a day for 40 days. See what happens.

This is not one of the eight limbs; it explains why these first two limbs are important and spells out how to practice the first two limbs. It acknowledges that there are things that happen to us (or thoughts that we have or feelings we get caught up in) that upset, distract, or constrict us. When we notice we are upset or constricted, we have another great opportunity to pattern interrupt and cultivate the opposite of whatever is going on for us.

There will be organic, moment by moment opportunities (as things come up naturally for us) to gradually create a new default setting for ourselves. We can change the way we react, respond, think, and are affected by our circumstances.

Today multiple studies have shown replacing negative thoughts with positive ones actually shifts neural energy from the hindbrain to the pre-frontal cortex. This takes us from "flight and fight" into the "rest and digest" function of our parasympathetic nervous system, slowing our heart and respiratory rates and synchronizing the function of our automatic, nervous and immune systems.

"Pondering upon the opposites" may very simply mean meditation, as some sutra scholars have interpreted. Except that meditation has been defined as the nullification of obstacles rather than the opposite of obstacles, and the word "bhavanam" (pondering, cultivating, realizing, dwelling on) is mental activity (as defined in sutra 1:6). So, those sutra scholars are wrong. . . (a little levity here)!

This is an important distinction because so many yogis believe that "thinking" is bad, that we should fear thought. Instead, this sutra advises us to think ON PURPOSE. Because thought happens. Rather than ignoring thoughts or resisting thoughts, this sutra suggests we should attend to thoughts. Cultivate awareness of what goes through the mind, decide if it is "true" and if it is not, to deliberately train the mind to think differently by dwelling on the opposite of that thought.

Thinking isn't bad or wrong. It's mind activity. It just is.

Unconscious thinking, however, may cause suffering. Awareness of thoughts and what motivates them starts the unbinding process. Deliberately reviewing "continuous loop" thoughts de-programs the mind. THIS IS A POSITIVE OCCURRENCE. Replacing thoughts that cause suffering with thoughts of the opposite is still thinking, without causing more suffering.

#20 sauca

2:40 Practicing purity weakens your identification with your body and distances you from others' bodies.

2:41 Moreover, through the practice of sauca, the subtle body is also cleansed, allowing for more clarity, joy, mastery over senses, ability to concentrate, and realization of self.

As my life started to become cleaner, I noticed that I had less identification with my physicality, as well as other mundane aspects of being in this body. I noticed that I did indeed have less appetite for mediocre food, mediocre sex, and mediocre relationships that would sully, or stand in the way of, my deeper experiences. This has allowed the meaning of purity to reach beyond the confines of my "skin" toward others outside of myself and toward my essence deep within. It feels like a deep respect for my body as the temple of my soul though; I don't feel disgust.

I know I am more than my body and I know everyone else is more than their bodies and it's a true gift to have that awareness. This very well may be the first step toward not fearing death, which is one of the klesas (root obstacles) that get in the way of yoga. So it holds value to me for that reason and makes sense as a BENEFIT in that context.

For someone starting off a yoga practice, purifying the mental layer of the subtle body is both sound advice (eat better, get rid of unnecessary messes in your surroundings, be cleaner in your thinking and your words, cultivate a less cluttered mind) and the result of the yoga (you will want to eat cleaner, your house will seem to stay organized, you will gain more clarity in your life, you do prepare your mind for the more subtle forms of yoga to come).
This practice creates a receptive vessel of your physical body (2.40) and your subtle body (2:41) and prepares both body and mind to receive the benefits of the practices that follow (sutras 2:42 – 3:3). In short, when you cleanse and purify, you create space.

The ways you can practice cleanliness are too numerous to list here. I'd start by simply looking around you; find ways to make cleaning a ritual and a spiritual offering. De-clutter your surroundings. Wash those dishes in the sink. Designate teeth cleaning time as sacred time. Clean up your relationships, etc.

Again, this is not a commandment. Just a different way to approach daily cleaning habits, and a conscious decision to "make space" for potential. The result of aiming for greater purity, both physically and energetically, is more clarity, joy, and preparation for the sutras that follow.

Here are three of my favorite "cleaning" habits that have proven effective and easy to incorporate into a busy life:

1.   Every night, make sure that before you go to bed you clean up and de-clutter your surroundings. If you do this nightly, this practice won't take more than five minutes. Make sure that if nothing else, the space around you is clean before you go to sleep. Then consciously tell your mind to cleanse itself while you sleep. Give your mind permission to show you all the things you need to sweep away while you're in dream-time. An easy way to purify the mind.

2.   Every day, do something that makes you sweat while practicing deep breathing. Even if that means you go to the sauna and do five minutes of ujjayi breathing while you bake. This is an easy way to cleanse the body.

3.   When you can, get as naked as possible in the sunshine, practice skin breathing while bathing in the sun. Lie down (on the ground if possible or on a chaise lounge). Close your eyes and start breathing the largest in-breaths possible. Imagine you are breathing directly through the pores of your skin. Pause at the top of the in breath and hold for a moment. Then imagine exhaling through the pores of your skin, as though you're cleansing every cell. Do this for at least five minutes, daily if possible.

#21 santosa

2:42 (Contentment): As a result of contentment, true joy (happiness, bliss, comfort) is attained (gained, achieved).

Practice being at peace with what is *and* what is not. This will reset your default state to joy. Other words for contentment that may make more sense are equanimity, tranquility, or acceptance of the way things are. Santosa is a reminder to be okay with where you are in your practice and life today. It is both sound advice – be at peace with what is – and a benefit of your practice. You really will acquire the unique trait of equanimity – the ability to slow down your reaction/response time so that you get to CHOOSE how to respond to different situations.

I spent most of my life believing I needed to better myself. Change myself. Improve myself. Then I started paying attention to when I feel the most at ease in my body and the people I am the most relaxed around. I'm drawn to people who are easy on themselves and others. Who don't question their worthiness, have nothing to do with the yoga industrial complex, have never bought a self-help book. I'd rather be on the beach with a good book and a nice shot of tequila, a cigar and some good music, than attend another superiority seminar masked as "help."

I'm good. You're good. I don't need help being myself. I am myself. And I love the energy surrounding people who are themselves. I am not suggesting we should all become lazy slobs! Conscious contentment is not laziness, nor is it something we can fabricate. It comes from truly knowing who we are, which makes it okay to be where we are on the "spirituality spectrum."

To practice tangible contentment:

1.   Lie down on a yoga mat, or the ground, or your office floor, or a chaise lounge on the beach. Spread out on that surface, close your eyes, and turn your palms face up in the "mudra of receptivity." Make of your hands two "vessels" by keeping all of the fingers slightly upturned and joined; fold the thumb in close to the outer edge of your palm.

2.   Intend to keep the hands in this mudra throughout the exercise. Intend to lie still with your eyes closed. Repeat the mantra, silently or quietly: "I am open and receptive to all experience."

3.   For the next five to ten minutes, simply be present to any experience that comes your way. Intend to lie still.

4.   If it's uncomfortable, practice being present with the discomfort. Notice you really are okay even if you're experiencing discomfort. Repeat the mantra and check in with your mudra – make sure the hands are still cupped with palms upturned.

5.   If you move or your mind wanders, practice being present with the movement. Notice you cannot be changed by any physical or mental movement. Repeat the mantra and check in with your mudra.

6.   If you feel incredibly relaxed and open, practice being fully present with the relaxation. Notice that even this relaxed state requires receptivity. Repeat the mantra and check in with your mudra.

7.   If you're in the sun and you start to sweat, or in an air-conditioned office and you start to shiver, practice being present with those sensations, noticing that nothing need take away your contentment.

8.   To end the exercise, acknowledge that nothing has happened that could lead your soul to a state of discontent. Then get up, stretch a little, and go about your business, receptive to all of the experiences the rest of the day affords you.

#22 tapasah

2:43 Asceticism: Through fiery self discipline the body and senses are perfected and special powers are attained.

This may be a quality of the person who is drawn to yoga, it is definitely a quality needed if we want to stay committed to yoga, and more often than not it is a result of doing the yoga. Tapas reminds us that we will need to make a commitment and have a burning desire to engage in a practice that might make us "weird" or "not normal."

Asceticism is both the fire that dissolves all the aspects of whom we are not, and a burning desire to connect with whom we truly are. This may mean we party less, are less popular, make less sense, or seem less fun, but we don't care because we yearn to know our Self more.

Tapas is one of my favorite niyamas because it implies a fiery passion to connect to something higher. It definitely lets the practitioner know that life does not have to become mediocre, boring, dull, or austere. It guarantees I will become MORE alive, more awake, and more courageous; plugged into a deeper power source.

I experience Tapas when attending a challenging asana class, especially when I commit to going on a regular basis.

For this particular niyama practice, challenge yourself to find a new yoga studio and commit to attending a yoga class every day for a week. Mix in some restorative classes but definitely take challenging classes as well. If you're already past that point, commit to doing a physical yoga session every day for a month. Get out of your comfort zone, stay fiery in your commitment, generate some heat, and see what happens!

#23 svadhyaya

2:44 Niyama four, Svadhyaya (Study of the Self): Through study of sacred texts, self study, and/or recitation of mantra, you'll be brought into union with the God you worship.

Self-inquiry, mindfulness, self-study, searching for the Unknown (divinity) in the Known (physical world) are all aspects of this practice.
Simple ways to incorporate this niyama into your life:

1.   Study the teachings of more masters. Read more scriptures. Research the life of the sages, saints, and gurus. Just by focusing your free time on learning more about holy women and men, you're sending a clear message to your Self and psyche.

2.   Practice witnessing your life. Spend time paying attention to you. Imagine taking snapshots of moments with your mind's eye, rather than more instagramming and facebooking. Do so with objectivity and compassion. You're not judging. Just observing with curiosity.

3.   Listen to your thoughts and hold them up to the light of presence. We covered this in earlier exercises, but it bears repeating.

4.   Repeat the mantra OM often throughout your day. This was listed in chapter one as well.

This is fairly straightforward both as good advice and as a benefit of practice. Because you practice yoga, you're drawn to sacred texts about yoga. Because you study the sutras or other texts, you experience unity more and more with Self, with Isvara, with God. And because you're naturally aligned with your essence, you're going to be more attracted to forms of learning that uplift and edify your essence.

The most powerful form of svadhyaya that I've experienced is Vipassana Meditation, especially during a ten day silent retreat. I cannot recommend it highly enough; it's not hard to learn and it's got gentle aspects to it.

I cannot warn you enough; it's extremely thorough and will expose you to You. Vipassana is a Buddhist form of meditation, wherein the practitioner is directed to examine certain aspects of her/his own human existence while being trained to tune in to senses we've long ignored, thoughts we've pushed away, and identities we've embraced that no longer serve us.

Simply, vipassana trains the practitioner to listen to the machinations of the mind without getting caught up in the machine. It isn't pretty, but it is self-study of the most honest order.

If you feel so inclined, search out the dhamma.org organization to learn this method of meditation, and perhaps find a silent retreat to attend.

#24 ishvara pranidhana colors

2:45 Through total surrender to God, Samadhi is attained.

This practice was first taught to me by Ana Forrest and is a variation on Metta (loving-kindness) meditation. I've added to it over the years to create a powerful visualization exercise; you'll need someone to lead you through it or download it off my website!

1.   Start by lying down; make sure you are comfortable and warm. Close your eyes, visualize your spine.

2.   Bring your attention to the tip of the tailbone, and imagine fastening a red ribbon to the tip of the tailbone. Now infuse this ribbon with a feeling of unconditional love you've felt from another person. Wrap the red ribbon around your entire spine from the tip of the tailbone all the way up to the inside of the crown of your head. Fasten this red ribbon, infused with unconditional love, to your crown.

3.   Bring your attention back to the tip of your tailbone. Imagine fastening an orange ribbon to the tip of the tailbone. Infuse this orange ribbon with unconditional love you feel toward another person. Then wrap this orange ribbon, full of love you feel toward someone, around your spine, from the tip of the tailbone to the crown of your head. Fasten this orange ribbon to the inside of the crown of your head.

4.   Bring your attention back to the tip of your tailbone. Imagine fastening a yellow ribbon to the tip of the tailbone. Infuse this yellow ribbon with love you feel for yourself. Then wrap this yellow ribbon of self-love around your spine, from tailbone to crown, feeling the spine being wrapped in self-love. Fasten this yellow ribbon right inside the skull at the crown chakra.

5.   Come back to the tip of the tailbone. Imagine fastening a green ribbon to the tip of the tailbone. Infuse this green ribbon with compassion

toward someone with whom you have unresolved issues. Then wrap this green ribbon around your spine from tailbone to crown. Wrap your spine in the feeling of love for someone you're struggling with. Then fasten that ribbon full of compassion to the inside of the crown of your head.

6.   Bring awareness once again to the tailbone. Now fasten a sky blue ribbon to the tip of the tailbone. Infuse this blue ribbon with a feeling of appreciation for the life you've been given. Wrap this blue ribbon of appreciation around the spine. Fasten it to the crown.

7.   Come back to the tailbone, and picture a dark blue, indigo colored ribbon. Attach this indigo ribbon to the tip of the tailbone. Introduce the feeling of love for your community, your family, your friends, your sangha into this indigo colored ribbon. Wrap this indigo ribbon, full of connection to your community, around the spine. Fasten the ribbon to the crown.

8.   Come back to the tip of the tailbone with your attention. Picture a violet ribbon, and imagine fastening this ribbon to the tip of the tailbone. Infuse this ribbon with love for your God, your Source, the Divinity within. Fill this violet ribbon with that feeling and wrap it around the spine, from the tailbone to the crown. Feel the feeling of love of source being wrapped around the spine. Eventually, fasten this ribbon to the inner crown.

9.   Finally, wrap your spine in a white ribbon infused with a feeling of divine love. Feel what it feels like to be loved by Source, and make that into a ribbon of white. Take this white ribbon of divine love all the way up to the crown of your head.

10. For the last few minutes, anchor your gaze on your spine. Stay in your body, feeling the feelings, seeing the colors, and experiencing whatever there is to experience. When you feel complete, roll to one side into a fetal position, feel reborn, and after taking a few breaths there, sit up and chant OM at least seven times.

According to the Upanishads, Isvara means "a state of collective consciousness" – not someone we should worship but a state we can all tap into. Isvara is pure Spirit, and is a model for who the yogi can become. The yogi attempts to be as Isvara in the world. Thus, if Isvara is a source of unlimited possibility, pranidhana is an absolute giving over to unlimited possibility. A part of us (the limited, individuated part) must live in the world, but by surrendering to this higher potential (the unlimited, un-individuated part), we will not be absorbed by the world; instead, we will be absorbed by our higher potential.

#25 old and new brain

Yamas and Niyamas direct us to transcend the processes of our older brain. Practicing moment-by-moment non-violence (ahimsa) trains the mind to overcome the fight or flight response. Practicing moment-by-moment non-grasping (aparigraha) trains the mind to have greater impulse control. Practicing moment-by-moment non-using (brahmacharya) curbs the reflexes of reptilian brain. Practicing moment-by-moment non-lying (satya), non-stealing (asteya) and behaving cleanly (Niyama) trains the mind to utilize the pre-frontal cortex more; choose primitive behaviors less.

The Yamas predict how the reptilian brain will react to stimulus, and provide a very simple way to "choose differently." The Niyamas exercise and engage the most evolved portions of the brain.

A fun and funny practice that you can do anytime and anywhere (I engage in this one while driving) is what I've deemed "old or new brain?" Simply watch your reactions and responses to events around you and within you. Label them either "old brain reaction" or "new brain response." Don't analyze beyond that. Don't try to change your behavior in any way. Simply notice what you are doing in the moment and sort that behavior into one of two baskets. The old brain basket or the new brain basket. It is fun, interesting, and educational.

#26 asana

2:46 Asana is that which is steady and easy, stable and comfortable, firm and pleasant, firm but relaxed.
2:47 Asana is mastered when all effort is relaxed and the focus shifts to the Infinite.
2:48 When this is attained, opposing sensations cease to torment.

Judith Lasater translates sutra 2:46 as "Abiding in ease is asana." My friend and esteemed colleague Charlotte Bell writes that asana is "a constant play between the sluggishness of sloth and the brittleness of over-effort." These are, of course, more literal translations of the term asana. For accuracy though, asana is a *state* of balance, not a posture.

However, recently the term *asana* (and the third limb) has become synonymous with "yoga poses." Asana practice has come to mean the physical practice of moving the body through a series of positions to affect all systems of the body. These movements support the health of the body you're in, training the body to be both strong and flexible, both stable and soft, both solid and fluid.

Often times "purists" will state that people doing "asana" are not doing "real" yoga. As you've probably heard many times, most yogic scholars interpret the word *asana* as "prepare to take a seat." Expanding on this interpretation, these physical movements prepare the body for stillness. Once the body is brought into balance, it is ready to sit still and experience these non-movement oriented forms of practice.

I do not hold the opinion however that more physically challenging poses are less "yogic." The physical practice of Yoga is a phenomenal workout. If our intention is to get stronger, more flexible, increase our lung capacity, energy and endurance, aren't we exploring the potential of our body? And isn't that what Yoga is? Exploring potential?

I would argue that the physical practice has the potential to invite and evoke the experience of yoga, but it is not ALL that is Yoga. What concerns me is that when we keep trying to dress up the physical poses -- with inspirational quotes, preaching, weights, high temperatures, loud music, beer, wine, cannabis, goats, pigs, essential oils, acrobatics, laser light shows, fireworks, orgies, or whatever else you've seen offered lately -- it MAY distract us from going further, or even turn us OFF of the more subtle observances. Making asana the "be all/end all" hinders the desire to actually explore some of these deeper practices. If we could stay with the simplicity and the science of yoga poses, we'd find that they prompt us to move beyond them. These simple movements invite us to feel the tangible expression of presence, but the poses aren't meant to be the stopping point.

The physical practice of asana can provide a private, safe arena to practice listening. Move deeply into a yoga pose as a way to call to the surface your deep internal wisdom. Tap into your innate intelligence. Notice how your focus shifts from the physical effort to infinite potential. It is more transformational than it seems.

If you're new to asana practice, find a studio near you and sign up for their introductory special; they usually have one, so ask if it isn't advertised.

If you are a seasoned asana practitioner, go for the deeper meaning of this sutra. In every yoga pose, and indeed throughout your day, seek balance. Feel your way through each pose; intend both stability and comfort. Check your breath; ensure your breath is both steady and relaxed. Check your attitude; balance moving beyond your comfort zone with being kind to yourself.

#27 directed breath

2:49 Next is Pranayama.

This practice tangibly connects us to the relationship between body, breath, and consciousness:

1. Take any yoga pose you'd like, as long as it provides you with sensation. Notice where the sensation is specifically, and begin directing your attention to that area of your body.

2. Once your attention rests on the sensation, begin sending your breath there. Watch the inhale come through the nostrils to travel through the throat toward the sensation. Notice how it fills up this part of the body with awareness.

3. Practice until you actually feel that body location inhaling with you.

4. Try a different pose if you'd like, one that gives you some sensation. This time, imagine the sensation taking a breath independently of the nostrils and the breathing apparatus. Intend to breath directly to and from the area you sense.

5. Take one more pose if you'd like to switch positions. See if you can feel your whole body breathe with you, as if every cell breathes with you.

All pranayama exercises give us the opportunity to dance with our breath, interact with our breath, and get to know our unique breathing patterns better. In fact, conscious breath is the connection between the mind and the body. When we breathe consciously, we intentionally flood our system with concentrated awareness.

#28 antir kumbhak

2:50 Breath modification is three-fold: external (exhale), internal (inhale), and motionless (held). These modifications are regulated by place, duration, and amount. These modifications are either long or short.

Pranayama is conscious regulated breathing. It is a science; a very precise way of changing patterns. Pranayama takes the mind off autopilot. It takes a completely unconscious autonomic process – breathing – and makes it conscious. Unconscious breathing is regulated by the medulla oblongata, the reptilian brain. By consciously controlling our breath, this autonomic function is directed away from the reptilian brain, now requiring the engagement of the frontal lobes.

This sutra states that there are three parts of the breath we can alter. We may modify the exhalation, modify the inhalation, or modify the space between the exhale and inhale (the emptiness and the fullness). We may breathe to different places in the body; may take longer or shorter exhales, inhales, or holds. And we may vary the number of repetitions for each exercise, and the number of holds we place within those exercises.The following practice is one of MANY commonly referred to as "kumbhak" or "retention" breath:

1.   Start with ujjayi breathing. If you're unfamiliar with ujjayi, it is a breath you take through the throat. To find it, start humming while you exhale, but continue humming as you start your inhale. You'll feel the throat constrict, hear the sound of the inhale moving across the larynx, and notice the inhale slow down. To keep ujjayi going on exhale, imagine you're trying to fog up a mirror as you whisper "hah" through the mouth. You'll feel the throat widen and the abdominal muscles engage. Now do the same but with the mouth closed. That's the ujjayi exhale.

2.   Lengthen the duration of your inhale to at least three seconds. Bare minimum. Then match the duration with your exhale. Take ten breaths this way, gradually growing the duration of your inhale to at least five seconds. Make sure your exhale matches the duration of your inhale.

3.   After ten repetitions of ujjayi breathing, add a hold at the top of your next inhale. Hold the breath for the same amount of time it took you to inhale. Then exhale for the same duration. Repeat this ten times: inhale, hold the in-breath, and then exhale. Make sure the ratio is 1:1:1.

4.   Once you're adept at holding the inhale side of the breath, begin to hold the in breath for double the duration of the inhale. Repeat this ten times: Inhale, retain in-breath, exhale with a ratio of 1:2:1.

5.   Then take at least three rounds of ujjayi breathing without any holds.

6.   Let the breathing normalize and simply sit quietly, noticing whatever there is to notice, for at least another minute.

#29 bahir kumbhak with bandha

2:51 There is a fourth stage of pranayama which takes us beyond the domain of exterior and interior. It is a continuous flow that surpasses the outer and the inner realms.

Pranayama could also be referred to as the art and science of stepping into the continuous flow of Prana (the life force). Being in the "flow" assimilates concentrated amounts of energy (prana), feeds the breath layer of the subtle body, and stimulates the autonomic nervous system. We are energetic beings; our energetic body receives the nourishment of prana through these practices just as food fuels our muscles and brains.

At this fourth level we learn about a flow state available to us beyond the action of breathing in and out. The flow that exists in the "void" of not breathing. Many yogic scholars interpret this stage specifically as the hold at the end of the out breath, while empty. More accurately, the experience we have during that moment of "without." This is the space where the most potential lies for activating, channeling, and consciously utilizing prana. This is the "aha" moment we strengthen within us when we spend time in the space between our out breath and the next in breath.

There's also good physiological benefit to exhaling fully and completely, even if you only hold for a second. Without training your breathing muscles to support complete exhales, carbon dioxide (a stressor) remains in your lungs, taking up space we need for oxygen. Conversely, when you exhale completely, you expel much more carbon dioxide, and allow your body to take a "reflex" inhale. The full exhale engages the internal intercostal muscles, which knit the ribs in and down. This action wrings out all stagnant air from the lungs to creates a partial vacuum, the perfect scenario needed for a full inhale to occur - as a neurological reflex - on its own. You've made room for more air, which brings in more oxygen, which alone will vastly increase the quality of your life.

The following exercise will teach the muscles of the exhale to move more carbon dioxide out of the lungs, massage all of your internal organs, and get stronger. You'll reduce stress levels and notice greater energy as well:

1.   Sit in a chair with spine upright and extended. Set a timer for at least ten minutes (20 – 60 is powerful). Place your hands on the sides of your ribs. Gently push your ribs down and in as you exhale. Continue exhaling until there is nothing else to wring out.

2.   Now pause, without allowing the in breath to rush in. Draw your navel back and slightly upward with a deep abdominal contraction. Keep your spine extended and chest open. Hold for a moment, feeling your abs engage and your throat "lock." If you know uddiyana bandha and jalandhara bandha, take those now.

3.   When you decide to take the next inhale, let go of the contractions in the throat and belly first, then let the reflex inhale happen. Feel (with your hands still on your ribs) how the ribcage moves up and out, as the reflexive action of the inhale takes place. You can drop the arms alongside your torso at any time.

4.   On the next repetition, count how long it takes you to exhale. Intend to lengthen the duration of the out breath to at least ten seconds (this may take some time). If you feel empty before the count of ten, just keep the action of the exhale going without letting an inhale happen. Hold at the end of that long exhale for the same duration (gradually grow this hold to match the duration of your exhalation if it causes you any discomfort or anxiety). Engage the bandhas if you know them, including mula bandha.

5.   Each time you are ready to inhale, release the inner muscular contractions first. Intend to slow down the inhale to match the duration of the exhale.

6.   Practice for a minimum of ten minutes. Upon completion, let the practice fall away and sit quietly, aware of any changes or differences you are feeling after this exercise.

#30 sushumna wash

2:52: Once you tap into that continuous source of prana, the cloud that has been obscuring the light melts away.
2:53   And the mind becomes ready to concentrate.

When you experience pranayama, you realize that it very quickly quiets the mind. After a few repetitions, you'll notice you do step into a void; or, more accurately, you'll acknowledge this "emptiness" or "openness" even after you finish your practice. Pranayama makes space for the mind to ready itself for concentration.

My family has a cabin where we gather each spring, after the winter thaw. The first thing we do when we arrive is open all the windows and the doors, so that the spring breezes can sweep out the trapped air in the cabin, and the sunlight can flood in to purify the space as well.

Pranayama is the clean, crisp, spring wind that removes the stagnancy of a long winter of inner neglect. It opens the inner windows to allow the light to flood in. This is an observation as much as it is a promise; the earliest yogis noticed this "side effect" and recorded it here. They experienced it as a powerful tool; one that makes this "quest for Self" more accessible.

This specific breathing practice clears the cobwebs, the dust, the murkiness away, leaving us with a bright light and clear view of the inner landscape:

1.   Sit on the ground, preferably on earth, in a meditation pose; stay upright.

2.   Close the eyes and imagine gazing up at the crown of your head with your third eye. Keep the physical eyes relaxed. Imagine creating a small opening at the top of the head. Place an imaginary funnel in the opening.

3.   As you inhale, focus your attention above the funnel. Intentionally vacuum the air through the funnel, through the crown of your head, and down to the top of your spine.

4.   As you exhale, intentionally plunge the breath down the length of your spine until you reach the tailbone. Imagine the smallest opening at the tip of your tailbone; move the exhale out and down, into the earth beneath you.

5.   Bring your attention back up to the crown of your head. Allow the breath to become as subtle as it wants to be. As you inhale, intend to bring pure concentrated life force (prana, chi, or ki) through this funnel, through the skull, to settle at the top of the spine.

6.   As you exhale (can be a very subtle exhale) plunge the breath slowly down the spine. I like to imagine a French press coffee maker here. Move the breath out of the opening at the tailbone and follow the pathway of the exhale into the earth.

7.   Keep this going for at least ten repetitions. Then allow the mind to rest in a state that is ready for concentration. When the mind gets fidgety again, start at the crown of your head (go back to #3) and begin again.

8.   Take conscious breaks from the exercise so you can fully experience the light within and the settled mind that has been prepped for concentration.

9.   When you feel complete, Take your attention back up to the top of the head Imagine removing the funnel; close up the opening in the crown. Take your attention down to the tip of the tailbone. Imagine sealing up the opening there. Sit quietly for at least five minutes, physical eyes relaxed, eyes closed, looking for any evidence of light radiating from within the body or behind the eyelids.

#32 pratyahara mudra

2:54 When the sense organs withdraw themselves from their respective objects and thus begin to imitate the mind, this is pratyahara.

This requires the use of another mudra, which I call the pratyahara mudra. This enables the practitioner to disengage from sensual perception while cultivating the ability to perceive of the inner world.

1. Do this lying down or seated. With your hands in front of your face so that you can see your palms, take your thumbs to your ears, place your index and middle fingers lightly across your closed eyelids, ring fingers under your nostrils, and pinky fingers over the outer edges of your lips. Use your thumbs to close off the ears so you dull outer sounds.

2. Begin ujjayi breathing. Refer to practice #27 to learn ujjayi breath. Listen to the breath move through the body. Watch the pathway of the breath within the body. Feel the breath move through the body.

3. Gaze at any colors, light, or other images that may appear in front of the minds eye.

4. Feel any warmth, heat, tingling, magnetism, or other sensations that may occur.

5. Listen to the heart beating, the stomach churning, the breath continuing, and whatever else you can hear within you.

6. When the arms get tired, release the mudra but continue the exercise. Resume the mudra when and if you need to.

7. When complete, lie down, spread out into a five-pointed star position, and simply notice how you feel for just a few more moments.

#33 pratyahara primer

2:55 Then follows a supreme ability to control the inclinations of the senses.

On a very practical note, the following easy exercise cultivates and supports a person's ability to engage innate intelligence in decision-making. The conscious mind becomes the central base of operation and is equipped to withstand outer influence. I have taught this to many of my clients in high-powered, high-stress careers and they swear by it. Sometimes simple just works.

Close your eyes. Bring your attention within.

See with the mind's eye. Realize and repeat: All sights are within me.

Listen with the inner ear. Realize and repeat: All sounds are within me.

Feel with the subtle body. Realize and repeat: All feelings are within me.

You may taste or smell subtle aromas. Repeat: All That Is, is within me.

Experience first hand your inner colors, inner harmonies, inner spaces, inner timelines. Realize and repeat: Everything I need I sense within me.

Feel the quiet inner voice of beauty and remain in that peaceful place for a few moments.

Pratyahara quiets the autonomic and limbic systems by predicting what the distractions will be. It is the difference between our attention being pulled in ten different directions, and the practice of DECIDING where to place our attention. It is exercising our ability to dismiss the sound of traffic that may have completely consumed our attention in the past. It is choosing to listen to the sound of our heartbeat rather than the voices in our head.

Pratyahara teaches us that we are free agents; in a world that demands our attention we get to decide to what we attend. It proves that we are not our sensations, we are not our instinctual drives or sensual appetites.

Imagine your conscious mind as a celebrity at a party, and all of your senses as people vying for her attention. Admirers wanting an autograph, servers enticing her with platters of hors' d'oeuvres, a bartender shaking up the perfect martini, photographers snapping pictures, and children throwing a tantrum just for good measure. The practice of pratyahara gives the celebrity (the conscious mind) the authority and compassion to say to the attention seekers, "Excuse me folks, I'll be in the other room." Pratyahara gives the conscious mind a room of its own.

Chapter Three
Powers

All told, yoga could be described as spiritual technology designed to inhibit our autonomic systems. In other words, yoga helps us overcome the previous limits of our biology so that we can fully evolve as human beings.
~Danielle Prohom Olson

#33 Dharana (concentration)

3:1   **A. holding the mind upon an object.**
      B. binding the citta (mind stuff) to one place.
      C. when the attention is held to a single object or spot.

This straightforward practice is like exercise for your attention; it will strengthen your ability to find meditation.

1.   Pick an object. For example, my friend Stan wrote a whole book about listening to the ticking of a clock or the hum of the refrigerator as his object of concentration.

2.   Bind your attention to that object. Use your senses.

3.   Keep concentrating on the object. Use it as an anchor for your mind.

4.   When the mind wanders, bring it back to the object.

5.   Concentrate some more on that object of awareness.

6.   Eventually, you'll notice you spend less time wandering off and more time with the object.

By bringing all of your attention to any (gross or subtle) object--an apple, or the palm of your hand, or meditation beads, or the sound of chimes, or your breath--you'll have that object to attend to when the mind wanders. Because you've created an anchor for your attention, it doesn't float away entirely from the shore.

This work is effortful, but should not be forced. In other words, just sitting still with your eyes closed planning the menu for the boy scout picnic next week is NOT dharana. The exercise of bringing your conscious mind back to your anchoring object every time the thoughts of the picnic come into your head is dharana.

So let the thought come in, acknowledge it, and then re-find the object; focus back on the object. Notice another thought sprout up, and bring your attention back to the object to pull the thought out of the mind before it establishes roots. Eventually, you'll notice the impulse that generates a thought so that before the thought can even take shape you'll be back to the concentration exercise. Thus we stay at a deeper level of concentration, which eventually leads us right to meditation.

Dharana exercises and develops the mind by strengthening and reinforcing the use of the pre-frontal cortex of the brain; in effect, it trains the mind to utilize the most evolved part of the brain rather than relying on the autonomic and limbic systems. It is usually considered a preparation for meditation but is a powerful way to train the mind to respond intelligently rather than react with a fight or flight response.

Dharana also develops steady awareness so it trains the mind to be present more often. I teach attorneys and negotiators and people who have to go "argue their case" a simple technique of just paying attention to the palm of their hand while they're listening to their clients. It is a way to anchor presence and a way to stay out of that reactionary place so that decisions are made and advice is given from a place of greater intelligence and intuition.

#34 Dhyana (Meditation)

3:2 Sustained concentration, uninterrupted stream of attention, uninterrupted flow of the mind towards the object.

Dhyana marks the shift from the effortful work of sense withdrawal and concentration to the effortlessness state of meditation. Dhyana liberates our entire being from the fluctuation of the mind. That moment, during concentration -- perhaps fleeting at first -- when the effort of concentration falls away to leave you in essence, to experience perfect peace.

Dhyana is not an efforted practice – it is simply a quality of awareness that in its stillness embraces deep peace and vibrant joy. Without thinking about it. In this fleeting moment, there is an expansion into a different level of consciousness in which the energies of mind unite (no distractions getting in) to reveal their innate qualities, thus absorbing our attention fully. There is no way to deny the experience of it.

The "practice" of Dhyana then, is simply a continuation or by-product of Dharana. Concentrate on an object until you drop into that flow state, presence. The experience of unwavering attention is Dhyana.

One of my favorite meditations is to concentrate on the ocean until I feel absorbed in the wavelike undulating presence of the ocean. You could use a lake, a river, or any body of water; I've actually found it really powerful to meditate on bath water. One of my stranger and more memorable meditations happened in the bath, in fact. I truly felt absorbed and embraced by the water, as if my body was no longer bathing in the water but had melted into the water. Weird, but no joke. I like to meditate with water because it tunes me right into the flow state this sutra describes.

#35 samadhih

3:3 Samadhi (experience of deep absorption) is:
A. when awareness is unconscious of itself
B. experiencing essence, devoid of form; non-self
C. When that same awareness (from dhyana) is as if unbounded.

The direct experience of being "woven into the intricate matrix of creation;" at this point, there is no one meditating, no one concentrating, no practice, no exercise, only essence. This is where we tangibly and directly experience our limitless, divine, infinite nature.

This goes one step beyond stilling the fluctuations of the mind. This is where you spontaneously experience expansion and unity of your consciousness with divine consciousness. You experience the unbounded and infinite You.

There is no guarantee you will experience it; it simply happens when the conditions are right, and I have no idea how to gauge when those conditions are right. I have had the experience of Samadhi only a few times throughout my long connection with meditation. Once was on the beach in El Salvador, where I (without going into all the details) became absorbed into the ether around me, shiny and glistening, sparkly droplets of "me" became the air. Another time, during one of the lowest and most conflicted points in my life, I felt absolute sameness with all sounds around me; I was birdsong, I was wind in the leaves, of the trees, I was the sound of roots growing in the earth. I was all sound. I can't tell you how to make the conditions right. Don't look for it and don't expect it because attachment to any outcome will prevent Samadhi.

The formula:
Regular repetition of . . .

1. Pranayama to prepare the mind for concentration

2. Dharana to train the mind to sustain attention

3. Dhyana, the result of concentration

4. Samadhi, the by-product of dhyana

#36 generic sanyamah

3:4 Samyama/Sanyama is the three (dharana + dhyana + samadhi) practiced together on one object.

By practicing concentration (dharana), which leads you to the experience of meditation (dhyana), which leads you to awareness of "non-self" i.e. infinite pure potential, (samadhi), you move into sanyama; a power to direct your mind so completely toward an object that you possess the traits of that object.

More of an experience than a practice, this is what happens when you practice concentration, experience absorption, expand into unbounded potential, *with intention.*

The rest of this chapter provides sanyamas with specific intentions with which we can experiment.

The larger point to this sutra is that you want to hone the skills of dharana, be well versed in the absorption of dhyana and have prior experiences of samadhi to prepare your body and mind for the possibility of the specific sanyamas that follow.

#37 viloma

3:9 Nirodha Parinama is when the attention moves from the rise and fall of the mind's impressions to the silence in between impressions. When the mind is associated with the cessation of the fluctuations of the mind, it is in the state of nirodha parinama.

The first level of transition of consciousness is Nirodha Parinama: the awareness of the transition into suspension. Taimni, in his translation of the sutras, describes Nirodha Parinama this way: "That transformation of the mind in which it becomes progressively permeated by that condition [of emptiness] which intervenes momentarily between an impression which is disappearing, and the impression that is taking its place."
1:47 and 1:51 defined it as "when no more thought waves enter the mind." Or "devoid of even subtle thought." Nirodha Parinama is becoming witness to the space of TRANSITION from one thought to another thought; immersion into the lack of impressions between impressions.

Here's one version of Viloma Pranayama I love; a breathing practice that helps me tangibly connect to the space of transition between impressions:

1.   Find a comfortable seated position or, you can lie down for this one if you can stay awake.

2.   Start with Ujjayi breathing. Take three rounds of ujjayi breath. Maintain ujjayi throughout this exercise.

3.   Place your hands on the belly to help you find "belly breath." Begin to isolate the placement of the breath by breathing only to and from the lower belly; intend to fill up (and empty out) the pelvic cavity, lower abdomen, and lower back. Take at least three rounds.

4.   Move your hands up to your floating (lower) ribs to find "ribcage breathing." Place your thumbs on the back ribs, your fingers on the front ribs and let the palms rest lightly on the sides. Take at least three breaths to and from the floating ribs.

5.   Move your awareness up to your chest to find "clavicular breathing." Place the hands so that the thumbs touch the front of each shoulder and the forefingers rest on the collarbones. The other three fingers rest lightly on the upper thoracic ribs. Isolate your inhales only in the upper thoracic cavity, breathing to the chest, all the way up to the collarbone, and in the back, breathe into the shoulder blade area all the way up to the base of the neck. Take at least three rounds to and from only your chest.

6.   Let your arms rest by your sides. Take a strong exhale; hold empty for a moment, then inhale only to your lower abdomen. Pause for two seconds. Take a second inhale (without exhaling) into only your floating ribs. Pause for two seconds. Take a third inhale into only your chest. Pause for two seconds.

7.   Exhale for ten seconds (or more) until you are empty. Hold empty for a moment; begin again. Take at least ten to twenty rounds of this practice.

8.   Take three more rounds without any pauses, inhale to belly, ribs, chest. Exhale from belly, ribs, chest.

9.   Then take three more rounds of ujjayi breath without directing the placement of the breath.

10.   Let ujjayi fall away. Let all effort behind the breath fall away. For a few minutes notice the natural pause between inhale and exhale, and between exhale and inhale. Simply resolve to stay present for those transitions. Even if/when the mind wanders, resolve to come back to presence during that moment of transition.

11.   When complete, take some deeper breaths, open your eyes slowly, and stay present as you transition from this exercise to the next part of your day.

#38 maitryadisu balani – layered radiance breath

3:24 Practice samyana on love or friendship, and the power to transmit them is accrued.

These qualities will be yours to use once you have experienced the essence of them. As you train your attention to focus unceasingly on love, you will move toward it. As you form higher and larger conceptions of friendship, these elements will begin to find expression in your words, acts, character, person, talents, powers, attainments, and achievements.

Sutra 1:33 describes a similar practice; stating that we can concentrate on people who are friendly to experience friendliness, etc. This sanyama is concentration on the feeling itself, to have the power to transmit these feelings. The power to transmit love or friendship or joy implies that humans have the power to conduct love; a human radiating waves of love affects other humans as well.

This is the premise behind the Hearth Math Organization's hypothesis that when we give our full presence (practice sanyama) to feelings of friendship, compassion, love, joy, appreciation, and other similar emotions, those feelings radiate to every cell within the body, and beyond the skin into the field around the body. This transmission of electromagnetic energy is received by other bodies, and has (according to Hearth Math) a "measurable effect on other people." They have also attempted to prove that practicing presence on these powerful emotions while intending to tap into the potential locked into our DNA actually causes the DNA to unravel.

On a larger scale, Heart Math data suggests that we feed the earth's field, not just another person's field, when we activate feelings of love and friendship.

While – to date – their experiments don't meet all the criteria to prove their hypothesis, it blows my mind to ponder this sutra within the context of heart math's hypothesis. This sutra certainly suggests it's something with which to continue experimenting.

I highly recommend looking into what the Hearth Math Organization is attempting to prove; seems like common sense to me.

Here's a practice inspired by HMO's research:

1. Slow your breathing to at least three second inhales and four second exhales.

2. "Activate a positive feeling." Feel appreciation for a kindness recently offered to you, or love for a fellow human, or joy for the feeling of sunshine on your skin. Feel it, and then make sure your breathing matches that feeling.

3. Imagine that this regenerative breath originates at your heart center. Inhale and watch it expand from the heart into the spine and all of your internal organs. Exhale to return your attention and feelings to the heart.

4. Inhale and expand this tangible feeling of joy, appreciation, love, compassion, etc. all the way out into the skin. Exhale to return from the skin back to the heart.

5. Inhale and expand this positive feeling from the heart beyond the skin, around the body. Exhale and bring this positive feeling back to your heart.

6. Keep this going, further and further beyond the confines of your body to radiate this regenerative feeling into the world around you as you inhale, and back to your heart as you exhale.

7. Eventually reverse the process; breathe that energy closer and closer in, until you reach the skin, then the internal organs, then the spine, and finally rest back at the heart.

8. Drop all effort behind the breath and simply reside at the heart center, generating and cultivating these high-powered emotions, for just a few more moments.

9. When you're ready to move from this meditation, take some deeper breaths and some large movements to get back into your body.

#39 ajna chakra meditation

3:26 When you practice samyama on the inner light, you can see what is subtle, hidden from view, or far away. Far away and near will cease to exist for you.
[6th chakra, ajna, reference]

What is the inner light, and how do you find it? I've learned from Kriya yoga to look for it in the spine. In Reiki I've learned to feel it in my hands. You can also focus on your third eye center, with eyes closed, or gaze from your third eye center at anything within the body or even beyond the body.

This practice combines all three. Start with five minutes of this and work your way to fifteen minutes. It's very energizing and sometimes overwhelming.

1.   Lie down on a bolster or rolled up blanket so that your head is propped up and your back is supported. Close your eyes and resolve to keep your physical eyes relaxed.

2.   Cup your palms over your eyes. Point your fingers at the center of your forehead.

3.   Begin breathing in through the nostrils to draw the breath to the third eye (behind the center of your forehead). Exhale the breath down the spine, as though you're looking down at the spine from your third eye. Keep this going.

4.   When your arms get tired, let them rest alongside your torso.

5.   Without expecting anything to "happen," notice any evidence of light, electricity, energy, color, in the body or right there in front of the inner gaze. You may feel tingling, warmth, vibration, magnetism, heaviness or a feeling of floating as well. You may see what looks like a starry sky or you may see nothing. Don't expect anything and don't try to fabricate anything. Just notice any sensations, images, or energy. Bring all of your attention to that.

6.   When the mind wanders away from attending to this light, go back to the practice. Place the palms over the eyes, inhale through the nostrils toward the third eye center, look down at the spine with that inner gaze (keeping the physical eyes relaxed) and exhale down the spine.

7.   Again when you notice any evidence of light, make that sensation the object of your awareness until the mind wanders away. Begin the practice again.

8.   When you're complete, take the time to rest in savasana (lie prone on the floor or ground) for at least five minutes. Open the eyes slowly and blink a few times to transition.

#40 fire breathing

3:27 Through Samyana on the sun comes the knowledge of the world.

[3rd chakra, manipura, reference]

Some translators have decided that "surya" should be translated as "inner sun" rather than just "sun," arguing that at this level, sanyama is focused on the most subtle of experiences. So this sutra could be translated to mean, practice sanyama on your solar plexus to have knowledge of the world. With that in mind, I've chosen a breathing practice that stimulates the manipura chakra.

My favorite solar plexus breathing practice is Fire Breathing, from the Bishnu Ghosh tradition. I learned it when I was 22 years old at the end of my first Bikram class, and have been practicing it almost daily since then. I highly recommend this as a morning exercise, before you eat, or around 4 pm, when the doldrums have a tendency to kick in.

1.   The traditional seated pose for this is seated hero's pose, but you can sit on a block or bolster as well.

2.   Take a few deep breaths, to calm and prepare the mind.

3.   Take a large inhale through the nostrils, then exhale through the mouth. Do this three times, engaging your core muscle groups to help you move the last bit of exhale out of the body.

4.   Take another large inhale, this time exhaling forcefully (with the use of your abdominal muscles) and repeatedly, allowing the inhale to come in on its own. This is similar to bhastrika but the exhale happens through the mouth. Start with 30 repetitions and work your way up to 108.

5.   At the end of your round, take a long inhalation, hold the in breath for a count of three, then exhale easily. Do this once again. Pause without any effort or emphasis on breath; simply revel in the feeling this practice stirs up for you.

6.   When the mind begins to wander off, repeat the fire-breathing, inhale through the nose, then exhale from the abdomen. Feel the abs draw back toward the spine each time you exhale. Do another 30 – 108 repetitions.

7.   At the end of the round, take a full breath in, hold it for a count of three, then allow the exhale to be a simple letting go of the inhale. Repeat this once again, then allow all effort to drop away while you bring awareness to the results of the fire breath.

8.   Take a third round, ending with full inhales and settling into silence after the deep inhales. Stay as long as you are able in that state of silent presence.

9.   Avoid this practice if you are pregnant or if you have high blood pressure, hernias or ulcers.

#41 agni sara

3:30 From Sanyama on the navel chakra (nabhi-cakre) comes knowledge of the anatomy and organization of the body.

[2nd chakra, svadistana, reference]

We now know we can study anatomy and physiology books, or google this information. So maybe this one doesn't seem all that impressive. However, this sutra is referring to the energetic anatomy of the body as well as the physical organization; the pathways and channels of our nervous system and the complex circuitry of our subtle body. It is through deep meditation on the navel that these early yogis were able to map out the nadis, the energy channels in the body.

In the early 2000's I had to have my gallbladder removed. The stress of moving across the country with three children under six, my brother's death, and a long drawn out divorce went right to my gallbladder. After the surgery, my doctor gave me one of my favorite compliments of all time. He said, "Your insides are beautiful. All of your organs are exactly where they should be." I shared my secret with him; I credit this next practice -- Agni Sara -- with my beautiful insides.

This exercise and the preceding practice (fire breathing) are both extremely beneficial. They both help reverse the effects of gravity on the internal organs and prevent the collapse of the connective tissue and viscera housed in the abdominal and pelvic cavities. They both act as an activator and cleanser for the digestive and eliminative systems.

Agni Sara strengthens the muscles of the pelvic floor and the transverse abdominus. It works most core muscle groups, providing tremendous intrinsic support for the spine. It massages every internal organ and moves lymphatic fluid upward while increasing circulation to the reproductive and eliminative systems. It keeps our energy up and our emotions "up" as well, promoting vibrancy from within.

Ultimately, this practice helps us find a deep awareness of our navel chakra, the intention of this sutra. I've made this practice a daily routine. I rely on this practice to massage, cleanse, and purify my body from the inside-out, while helping to hold all of my internal organs in the right place. Practice this one first thing in the morning, on an empty stomach, daily.

1.   PHASE ONE: Start on your hands and knees, in a cat/cow position. As you inhale, extend your spine.

2.   Exhale through the mouth vigorously, with a "sh" sound, while drawing your sit bones toward your knees. Draw your lower belly in and up. While you're empty, hollow out the lower belly so that it becomes concave. Attempt to keep the chest and upper body still. Feel the muscles of the pelvic floor draw upward and tighten.

3.   Release the diaphragm. Inhale, pull the pelvis back away from the lower ribs, and hug your spine with your spinal muscles. Let the lower belly fill. Allow the contents of the abdominal cavity to "spill" toward the floor.

4.   Exhale through the mouth with the "shhh" sound, repeating step two. Hold empty for one to ten seconds. Hollow out even more by vacuuming the diaphragm up under the ribs. Repeat this six to ten times.

5.   ONLY WHEN you can comfortably perform this exercise should you move to the next level. When you feel ready:

6.   PHASE TWO: Stand up, take a deep inhale, then exhale through the mouth, leaning forward to rest your hands on your thighs with your knees bent. Your lower back will round but the chest will stay open. Challenge yourself to sequentially contract as you exhale. First the pelvic floor rises, then the transverse abdominus tightens across the pubic bone (as if you're cinching a belt over your hip bones). Next, hollow out the lower belly, then contract the abdominal wall and hug your ribs toward each other with your internal intercostals. Once you're empty, draw the diaphragm up under the ribs to concave even more. This should all happen in about one to two seconds. Hold empty once all of the muscles of your core are engaged.

7.   Then practice releasing the contraction in the opposite sequence on inhale. Release the diaphragm first, then inhale as you engage your external intercostals, your abdominal wall, your lower abs, and the pelvic floor as the inhale completes. Hold the inhale for a moment. Begin again with sequential exhale. Do at least six repetitions a day of phase two.

8.   PHASE THREE: On the hands and knees OR standing position from above: Take a deep inhale, then exhale through the mouth with a "shh" sound. Hold empty; draw the belly in and up (in the sequential way described above). WITHOUT INHALING, let the belly descend toward the floor. Quickly draw it back up, then allow the contents of the abdomen to drop toward the earth again. Repeat once more, then RELEASE THE CONTRACTION before you inhale.

9.   Take a few regular breaths, then begin again. Inhale through the nose, exhale with the "shh" sound strongly through the mouth. Hold empty, while drawing the lower abdomen in and up, then releasing it, in and up, release, in and up, release. Three times while empty.
10. Take a few regular breaths.

11. PHASE FOUR: Gradually increase the repetitions of this abdominal massage (while empty). Once you can do three repetitions easily, do six, then nine, then 12. Once you've mastered this level of agni-sara, you can do this all without exhaling through the mouth.

12. After your repetitions, take a meditation pose. Contemplate your navel chakra. It is now activated and energized and easily found by your attention. You may notice sensations, emotions, or old mentalities coming up to be acknowledged. This exercise churns stuff up and brings things to the surface. So take it in the proper phases for sure and always leave time to sit quietly with your second chakra.

Always take some regular breaths in between the agni-sara massage, and do not do this if you've just eaten. Do not perform this exercise if you have a hiatal hernia, an ulcer, are pregnant, or if you have high blood pressure. Many women do not like to practice this when menstruating.

#42 ujjayi with jalandhara bandha

3:31 From Sanyama on the hollow of the throat comes cessation of hunger and thirst.

[5th chakra, vishudda, reference]

About fifteen years ago, I read a story about Sri Pralad Jani, a 76 year-old yogi who had been observed by over 20 doctors and was able to prove he could survive without food or water for over ten days. This intrigued me, and ever since then I've periodically read many more verified cases of non-eating yogis (and other saints in all traditions). While a few have been proven to be faking (eating McDonalds in secret) there are still those who have mastered this technique.

Ujjayi breathing, with optional jalandhara bandha, will help you practice sanyama on the hollow of the throat, just in case.

1.   Place your index and middle finger at the soft part of the throat, (your suprasternal notch, located between the collarbones). Whisper (any phrase you'd like). You'll notice you're exhaling. Now inhale and keep whispering. You'll feel the throat constrict and the soft part of your throat retract. If this doesn't work, hum a tune while exhaling. Continue to hum as you inhale. This is the inhale side of ujjayi breath, the side we will focus on.

2.   As you exhale, engage your abdominals, relax the throat, and move the breath out.

3.   Focus on the inhale; draw the breath in with that "whisper" constriction. At the top of the inhale hold the breath. While the breath is held, intend to slide the roof of your mouth back toward the back of the throat. At the same time, vacuum the soft part of the throat back as well. Hold for just a moment. Exhale with ujjayi exhalation.

4.   Inhale with ujjayi, and count how long it takes you to inhale. Hold with jalandhara bandha for half the time it took you to inhale. Exhale with ujjayi for the same duration as the inhale. Without any effort behind the breath, bring all of your attention to the hollow of your throat for double the length of the inhalation. Ratio then is 2:1:2:4. For example, inhale for 8 seconds, hold the inhale with jalandhara bandha for 4 seconds, exhale for 8 seconds and practice dharana (concentration) on the lower throat for 16 seconds. Take at least ten rounds.

5.   End by holding your concentration at the hollow of the throat for as long as you're able. Gradually begin breathing deeply, shake your body out a bit, and go on with your day! See if you notice any changes to your appetite. . . .

#43 kurma nadya observance

3:32 From Sanyama on the "kurma nadi" comes steadiness, motionless, immobility.
[referencing the energy channel or vehicle upon which prana travels; follows the path of the bronchial tubes]

This suggests we have the power to stay completely still, to "freeze." I've certainly read about yogis who can make their bodies completely immobile. In some cases, they supposedly leave their bodies, which is why the body remains immobile. In other cases, their consciousness remains and they are aware of the temporary immobility. In other cases, it is said that the yogi has moved upward into the higher realms of consciousness while his body remains still in the pose of meditation. The only time I've felt anything close to this is during deep meditation, losing conscious awareness of the body.

This practice comes from Osho, who states: "By performing samyama on the nerve called kurma-nadi, the yogi is able to be completely motionless. Kurma-nadi is the vehicle of prana: breathing." The subtle energy channel is located 1" down from the base of the throat and loosely follows the path of the bronchial tubes. Osho continues, "… silently watch your breathing, not changing its rhythm in any way, neither making it fast nor slow, just leaving it natural and relaxed . . . simply watch it, you will become absolutely still. There will be no movement in you." How does this happen? According to Osho, " . . . all movement comes through breathing, prana. All movement comes through breathing."

So, very simply, silently watch your breath. Simply watch it. When the mind wanders, watch it again. Watch the pathway of the energy of the breath. Do this a few times a day.

#44 sahasrara chakra meditation

3:33 From Sanyama on the light emanating from the top of the head (crown chakra) comes sight of the "siddhas" (the perfected beings, the masters, the luminous ones).

[7th chakra, sahasrara, reference]

You'll be able to see angels, gods, goddesses, your spirit guides, and perfect beings. We know plenty of people who claim these abilities. And remember this is a list of potential powers that all humans have, so if even ONE human has experienced this, it is entirely within the realm of possibility that you too, one day, could have this same experience.

This exercise will help you locate and generate this crown chakra radiance:

1. Sit in padmasana or any other seated crossed legged pose. Close your eyes.

2. From the vantage point of a spot approximately six inches above your head, look down (with your mind's gaze) at the crown of your head. Imagine light emanating from the top of the head. Cultivate that intention and notice any heat or tingling at the crown.

3. Concentrate on any light you see or even the light you are imagining until the mind wanders. When the mind wanders come back to the practice.

#45 anahata connection breath

3:35 From Samyama on the heart comes the full understanding of citta (energy field called mind)

[4th chakra, anahata, reference]

This is a slight variation on the connection breath I teach at all retreats; I love putting on my very favorite song *Corazon* by Arno Elias to practice this for the entire song, then taking a seated position or lying down to simply concentrate on the heart. It's extremely powerful.

1.   Start standing with your hands in prayer position at the heart center.

2.   Inhale your hands (still joined in the Anjali mudra – prayer position) up from the heart, touching the throat, the third eye, and the crown lightly with the thumbs, and then all the way up until the arms are straight, pointing your fingertips toward the sky.

3.   Exhale the prayer position back to the heart, touching the crown, the center of your forehead, the small of the throat, to rest at the heart.

4.   Inhale, reach your arms out to either side of the room, stretching your arm span as wide as possible.Exhale bring the hands back to the heart center into prayer position.

5.   Repeat steps two through five, taking breaks if/when the arms get tired. Eventually, drop the exercise. Rest your attention on the heart.

When we put all of our attention on our heart center, this opens the communication between the heart and the brain. Their research shows that the most direct pathway to the most evolved part of our brain – the pre-frontal cortex -- is through our heart. I like to do this first thing out of bed, to wake up and move a little, but also to start the day out with a conscious heart to mind communication.

#46 udana vayu breath

3:40 Master the up breath (udana) and you can levitate.
[referencing the prana vayus – specifically udana vayu]

"Udana is the upward-moving breath, which directs the flow of prana from the lower to the higher planes of consciousness. An ascending and radiant force, udana vayu is responsible for taking the mind from waking to sleep and to deep sleep, as well as to higher planes of existence after death. It is active primarily in the region between the heart and the head, bringing prana to the energy centers deep in the brain." ~Sandra Anderson

We could interpret the sutra to mean that when we master the force of the upward and outward moving breath we have the ability to float above the ground. Perhaps the body feels weightless because it feels more like ether than body. One day, when you witness someone levitating, you'll know they've mastered udana vayu breath.

This practice will not teach you how to levitate! However, it will allow you to access the udana vayu. What you do with it after that is up to you.

1.   Take a seated meditation pose of choice. Place the hands with palm pointing upwards on the thighs or the knees. Take the Udana Vayu mudra with both hands. Bring your ring, index and middle finger together, bending them all to join the thumb. The little finger should be pointed straight.

2.   Start ujjayi breath, as described in practice #42.

3.   Focus your attention on the spine. As you inhale with ujjayi, picture the in-breath entering through the tailbone, and use the slow in breath to vacuum the breath up the spine until it arrives at the base of the skull.

4.   Exhale through the nostrils. Watch the pathway of the exhalation for as long as you can as it moves outside the body.

5. Bring your attention back to the tailbone. Inhale through the tailbone, drawing the breath up the spine to the base of the skull. As you exhale through the nostrils, watch the exhale for as long as you can as it moves beyond the body to join the ether.

6. Keep this going until you really feel the breath connect to the base of the skull.

7. When the practice of ujjayi breath gets in the way, allow the breath to become subtle. Continue inhaling your way up through the inside of the spine, and exhaling your attention out through the nostrils.

8. When focusing on the breath gets in the way of the essence of the exercise, allow your attention to rest on the hand mudras.

9. When you're ready to transition, release the mudra, relax the fingers and open your eyes.

10. Perform at least three rounds of simhasana, or lion's pose. (see practice #47 for more instruction).

#47 lion's breath

Lion's Breath (simhasana) should follow the above to balance the system, but can be performed without the above exercise as a way to clear any "stuck" energy around the throat chakra. If you're only doing Lion's breath, take at least ten repetitions.

Sit in vajrasana, or thunderbolt pose.

1. Inhale, then lean forward, open the mouth and stick out your tongue with a strong and audible "roar" as you exhale.

2. The louder the better, and the more you stick out your tongue the better. As you lean forward to land on your palms, you mimic the stance of a lion roaring.

3. Do at least ten repetitions. I like to do this in the car for some reason. Especially when I'm driving my son and his friends around.

#48 skin breathing

3:41 Master the mid-breath/nerve current flowing to the navel area (samana) and your body will shine with the radiance of a star.

"Samana vayu is a concentrating, absorbing, and consolidating force. Its main function is assimilation of prana in all its forms—like a power station, samana collects energy absorbed through breath, food, sensory perception, and mental experiences and processes it to empower all aspects of life." ~ Sandra Anderson

This "wind" is from the outside in – moving from the periphery to the center of the body, to be absorbed at the navel. This particular practice recharges the inner battery. It is all about the inhale side of the breath; let the exhale happen on its own without any effort behind it.

1.   Lie down on your back with your arms and legs extending as far away from each other as possible, in star position. Cover your eyes with an eye pillow if you have one; if not, use a towel. Make sure your palms are face up., with fingers in the samana vayu mudra. Bring all four fingers together. Bend them all toward the thumb so that the thumb touches the pinky and the forefinger as well as the middle and ring fingers.

2.   Bring your attention to your skin. Imagine that you could bypass your nostrils entirely to breathe directly through the pores of your skin. Start by breathing through the palms of your hands, imagining that the breath is moving into all the joints of the fingers and up to be absorbed by the wrists.

3.   Bring your attention to the soles of your feet. Inhale through the soles of your feet, imagining that the breath is moving into the toes and up to be absorbed by the ankles.

4.   Now, imagine that your forearms are taking an inhale. Move the inhalation directly through the pores of the skin of both forearms. Watch the breath be absorbed into the elbows. Do the same for the calves and shins, with the inhalation absorbed by the knees.

5.   Then bring your attention to your upper arms; inhale through the skin of the upper arms to be absorbed by the shoulders. Follow this with the thighs; breathe through the skin surrounding the thighs with the inhale absorbed by the hips.

6.   Next, inhale through the pores of the skin of your face. Let the breath be absorbed by the jaw. Inhale through the hair follicles, allowing the breath to be absorbed by the skull sutures.

7.   Move down to the pelvis with the breath, imagining the inhale filling the pelvic cavity as it draws through the skin. Watch the breath be absorbed by space between the tailbone and the sacrum.

8.   Move up to the neck and throat. Intentionally bypass the nostrils to breathe through the skin surrounding the neck and throat. The breath will be absorbed by the cervical vertebrae.

9.   Move to the lower belly (below the navel and above the pubic bone) and the lower back (the lumbar spine and lower thoracic vertebrae). Inhale directly through the skin and move the breath into the spaces between the vertebrae housed in this part of the body.

10.   Bring your attention to the entire rib cage. Pull the breath in through the skin surrounding your ribs and spine. Watch the inhale absorb into the spaces between the vertebrae of the upper and mid-thoracic spine.

11.   Finally move to the navel itself. Intend to breathe through the navel, with the breath expanding into – and being absorbed by -- every nook and cranny of the inner body. As though you're filling your entire body with breath, inhale through the navel and expand toward and into the confines of your skin. Imagine your body is a sponge; pour as much prana through the navel as possible and let the inner body absorb it.

12. Breathe into the navel for a few repetitions. Then drop the breathing altogether and simply notice any radiance. Concentrate on your hands, re-configuring the mudra, your feet, the crown of your head, all pulling energy in to be absorbed at the navel.

13. When you feel complete, come to a seated hero pose (virasana) or thunderbolt pose (vajrasana) and take one round of at least ten repetitions of bhastrika (see practice 49).

I believe that it is through paying attention to the inner body that we find "the light," the place where all the parts of ourselves meet and "combust." Those parts are our spiritual essence and our unique human consciousness, all the different sides to our personalities, as well as our shared human experience.

#49 bhastrika

Bellows Breath (bhastrika) should follow the above to balance the system, but can be performed without the above exercise as a way to ring out the inner "sponge" whenever you feel you've absorbed too much energy.

1. Bhastrika begins with a quick exhale through the nostrils, and a conscious inhale also through the nostrils. An entire cycle of breath (one deliberate exhale and one deliberate inhale) should last one second.

2. If you're only doing Bhastrika, do at least three rounds of at least ten cycles. Work up to more cycles but progress slowly, as this one tends to make practitioners hyperventilate.

3. Take three normal breaths and sit quietly for a minute or two (or five). Notice how you are feeling. Practice this in the middle of the day to gauge how much energy you absorb before trying it at night, but I find this breath puts me to sleep.

#50 ear breathing

3:42 From Sanyama on the relationship between the ear and the ether comes celestial or supernormal hearing.

I believe this sutra means particularly that you can hear the promptings of celestial beings: angels, saints, spirit guides, gurus, the holy ghost.

1.   Take a meditation pose or even sit in a chair. Close your eyes and make sure to keep the eyes relaxed.

2.   Start by inhaling and exhaling through the nose. For this pose you can use ujjayi breathing or your normal breath. It's helpful to start with ujjayi breathing to make the breath more tangible and easier to follow; eventually move to natural breathing so that the practice becomes more internal and subtle. After three to six breaths, take a strong exhale. Hold empty, resolving to stay present throughout the next cycle of breath.

3.   As you take your next inhale, watch the two streams of breath move through the nostrils to join at the center of your forehead. Pause for a split second, with your attention at 3rd eye, then exhale and watch the one stream become two as it moves through the nostrils out into the ether. Follow the pathway of the exhale for as long as possible. Do this twice more.

4.   After the third exhale, hold empty for a moment. Resolve to stay present. Make sure your physical eyes are relaxed. Inhale and watch the two streams of breath meet to become one at the ajna chakra. Pause for a moment. This time, send the exhale out through the ears. Watch the pathway of the exhale move in two equal and opposite directions through both ears. Follow the exhale out beyond the body.

5.   Inhale through the ears, watching the two streams meet to become one at the center of your forehead. Pause for a moment. Exhale the one stream from the forehead through the nostrils. Watch the one become two as it moves out through the nostrils. As before, follow the pathway of the exhale into the space around you for as far as your attention takes you. Keep this going, inhaling to watch the two streams become one at the forehead center, exhaling through both ears, inhaling to pull the breath back to meet at the third eye, exhale from third eye through both nostrils.

6.   If you've been engaging ujjayi breath, switch to normal breathing after three full rounds. If you've been breathing normally, allow the breath to become even more subtle. Continue inhaling through the nostrils, pausing at third eye, exhaling through ears. Inhale through the ears, pause at third eye, exhale through nostrils.

7.   After about 12 rounds total, rest your attention at the third eye. When the mind wanders, come back to the practice for one round, then rest your attention right in the center of your brain, directly behind the center of your forehead. Again, make sure you keep your eyes resting in their sockets.

8.   To transition, lie down, place your palms over your eyes to shut out all external light, and rest. If you practice this before sleep, now's the time to sleep. Otherwise, when ready to move on, shake out the hands, draw your knees into your chest, rock side to side, then rock forward and back, eventually rocking up to a seated position. Open your eyes slowly, blink a few times, and go take on the day!

This practice may be my favorite of them all. It cleanses and purifies the energy channels and is purported to stimulate the pineal gland. I love to practice this right before I go to sleep. I set an intention to work out some question I may have, and invariably have very vivid dreams. Try it for a week!

Chapter Four
Potential

At birth and throughout your childhood, your thoughts and feelings were more than likely expressions of your true self. Though you may have learned quickly that to speak and act in a certain fashion would win others' approval, you understood innately that you were no ordinary being. There are many ways you can recapture the authenticity you once articulated so freely. Meditation can liberate you from the bonds of those earthly customs that compel you to downplay your uniqueness.
~unknown

#51 I am that I am mantra

4:14 "Since the gunas work together within every change of form and expression, there is unity in all things." – Prabhavananda

All the differentiated "stuff" around us is made up of all the same undifferentiated "stuff"; thus everything is the same and all things are connected. Gunas are ingredients; all three ingredients are present in all objects to varying degrees.

The way they form together is how differentiation occurs; all expressions and transformations require a mixing of the elements. Ultimately though, the commonality of these elements or ingredients is prakriti, or undifferentiated matter. This explains dualistic monism; how unity and diversity can exist concurrently.

The "I am that I am" exercise helps the mental layer of our subtle body understand this concept.

1.   Set a timer for ten minutes. If you find that ten minutes is too arduous, set it for four minutes (1+1+1+1), work up to seven minutes (1+2+2+2), then do the full ten minutes (1+3+3+3).

2.   Sit upright so you stay alert.

3.   Begin with preparatory breath to concentrate the mind.

4.   After approximately one minute, inhale and say out loud "I AM."

5.   Exhale and say out loud, "THAT I AM."

6.   After three rounds, add an object, or a quality, or an affirmation to "I AM." For example, on inhale state, "I am the ocean" or "I am pure light" or "I am blessed."

7.   On exhale, say out loud "THAT I AM."

8.   After three minutes of stating "IAM THAT I AM" out loud, begin whispering "I AM _____" on inhale, and whisper "THAT I AM" on exhale.

9.   After three minutes of whispering, repeat the same mantra, but silently now and internally.

When the timer sounds, sit for at least a moment, allowing the exercise to drop away and simply notice the results of this practice. As always, take some active breaths and move around a bit to transition to the next part of your day.

#52 kaivalyam

4:34 Once the gunas settle, pure unbounded consciousness remains and is forever established in its own absolute nature. This is freedom. This is self-realization. This is Kaivalya.

There is nothing to achieve, nothing to build, and nothing lacking. Everything we seek exists as pure potential within us, available to us in the precise moment we need it. We are truth. We are freedom. And that's enough.

I've given you 52 observances, one per week, to try on and perhaps add to your routine. This fifty-second "practice," inspired by the last yoga sutra, is both a conclusion and a commencement.

I leave you with this challenge:

Every single day, for the rest of your life here in embodied form, make sure that you take at least one moment to acknowledge this truth. Identify with your Self, your Essence, your Absolute Nature. Salute the part of you that has always existed and will always exist. Acknowledge that trials will still present themselves, emotions will still arise, loss will continue to occur while also admitting that you still remain whole and unblemished. At least once a day, establish your consciousness in its true nature.

And LIVE. That's the only real thing on the to-do list. Live.

"Freedom is not the goal of the human soul, but its very nature. By nature the soul is free." – Neale Donald Walsh

References

https://insights.ovid.com/pubmed?pmid=16272874

https://www.ncbi.nlm.nih.gov/pmc/articles/PMC1361002/

Meditation experience is associated with increased cortical thickness

Philippot, P. & Blairy, S. (2010). Respiratory Feedback in the Generation of Emotion, Cognition and Emotion, Vl. 16, No 5 (August 2002), pp. 605-627. Or free at: http://www.ecsa.ucl.ac.be/personnel/philippot/RespiFBO10613.pdf.

https://www.ncbi.nlm.nih.gov/pmc/articles/PMC5787085/

https://www.frontiersin.org/articles/10.3389/fnins.2018.00004/full Toward a Neuroscience of Adult Cognitive Developmental Theory

https://www.ncbi.nlm.nih.gov/pubmed/21034792

Increased default mode network connectivity associated with meditation.

https://www.ncbi.nlm.nih.gov/pmc/articles/PMC2944261/?rf=30039&mc=NjM4ODAwOQ

Buddha's Brain: Neuroplasticity and Meditation

Neural systems for perceptual skill learning.

Poldrack RA Behav Cogn Neurosci Rev. 2002 Mar; 1(1):76-83.

http://www.lifesci.sussex.ac.uk/home/Zoltan_Dienes/Tan%20et%20al%20Mindfulness%20meditation%20and%20BCI.pdf

Effect of mindfulness meditation on brain–computer interface performance

Neural systems for perceptual skill learning.*Poldrack RA, Behav Cogn Neurosci Rev. 2002 Mar; 1(1):76-83.*

Long-term meditators self-induce high-amplitude gamma synchrony during mental practice.

Lutz A, Greischar LL, Rawlings NB, Ricard M, Davidson RJ

Proc Natl Acad Sci U S A. 2004 Nov 16; 101(46):16369-73.

Made in the USA
Middletown, DE
22 September 2019